THE RAINBOW COLLECTION

QUILT PATTERNS FOR RAINBOW COLORS

by JUDY MARTIN

M.O.M.

Moon Over the Mountain Publishing Company
in association with
Quilter's Newsletter Magazine

Quilt photography by Jerry DeFelice
Front cover design by Bonnie Leman

Introduction

Everyone loves a rainbow. We see it as a happy surprise. A promise. A gift. The rainbow lights up the vastness of the sky with its colorful display, and then lets us feel clever for having noticed.

Rainbows have inspired poets and writers throughout the ages. "My heart leaps up when I behold a rainbow in the sky!" wrote William Wordsworth. Lord Byron called the rainbow "...the evening beam that smiles the clouds away, and tints tomorrow with prophetic ray." Alfred, Lord Tennyson called it "Gleam upon gloom, bright as my dream." Samuel Taylor Coleridge wrote of the rainbow, "That gracious thing made up of tears and light."

The rainbow appears in folklore, proverbs, and religion throughout the world. Almost always, the rainbow is seen as a promise. In the Bible, it is the token of God's covenant to all living creatures, made to Noah after the flood. To the Hebrews, the rainbow is a sign that God has forgiven our sins. In English folklore, a pot of gold is said to wait at the end of the rainbow. "Over the rainbow" is a never-never land where dreams can come true.

The rainbow, besides evoking pleasant feelings, provides a naturally beautiful example for organizing colors. Artists in all media have explored the rainbow theme. Quilters, too, have discovered that the rainbow sequence makes a delightful premise for a quilt. The multitude of colors adds interest, and the blending provides order and dignity.

I've made a half dozen rainbow quilts of my own over the years—and designed them from time to time for *Quilter's Newsletter Magazine* and *Quiltmaker.* About a year ago, Bonnie Leman and I were discussing a rainbow-colored quilt that I was designing for *Quiltmaker.* We both liked the pattern, but we were a little worried that our readers would be unable to make the quilt because of the difficulty of finding—at any given moment—all the colors necessary. It was then that we decided to design The Rainbow Collection fabrics.

When I knew that quilters could be sure of having access to a perfect rainbow progression of fabrics, I let my imagination go in designing for rainbow colors. One idea led to another, and before I knew it, I had a book full of rainbow quilts. And here it is.

When Bonnie Leman and I began to see the wonderful things that could be made from 24 rainbow colors, we couldn't resist multiplying the possibilities by adding 24 darker tones to The Rainbow Collection of fabrics. With all 48 colors, there is beautiful blending as well as enough contrast to make just about any quilt pattern you desire. The darker colors were not yet in hand when the quilts were made for this book. However, the darker colors can be easily substituted for the lighter ones shown—even the numbers correspond. And I have given suggestions for mixing the darker tones with the lighter ones in a number of the quilts. Any of the quilts can be made from rainbow-colored prints or scraps, as well. You'll surely have a few ideas of your own. So why not get started exploring rainbow quilts? I'm sure you'll find your pot of gold at the end of your journey.

IMPORTANT INFORMATION ABOUT THE PATTERNS IN THIS BOOK

The piecing patterns in this book include cutting lines (solid), seam lines (dashed), and arrows to align with straight grain of fabric. Just ignore the cutting lines if you prefer to make traditional hand-piecing templates and add the seam allowance by eye later.

No turn-under allowances are given for the appliqué patterns. You will add the 3/16" by eye when cutting.

Very large pieces such as alternate blocks are shown in miniature with dimensions. For a few of the patterns on pages 41-42, the large background squares are not diagrammed separately, but the dimensions are listed. In all cases, these dimensions do *not* include seam allowances. Use graph paper to rule these patterns in the measurements given, adding seam allowances when you mark and cut your fabric.

Seam allowances (plus two inches extra length for insurance) are included in border strip measurements.

If we give just half of a large pattern piece, the center line is indicated with a dotted line. When making the template, simply trace around pattern, flip the tracing over, and align the dotted center lines. Trace around pattern again to complete template for whole patch. Quilting motifs are shown in position in each patch, where they are designated by dashed lines.

When our quilt specifications call for a pattern letter followed by an "r," you will need to reverse the pattern. That is, if the instructions call for 36 A and 36 Ar, mark the first 36 patches, then turn the template over to mark the remaining 36.

The block size listed for each pattern is the finished size from seam line to seam line.

A piecing diagram is shown for each block. The diagram shows the pattern pieces, lettered to match their full-size counterparts. The patches are separated into units so that you can easily see how to assemble the block. Numbers indicate colors. The same numbers are used in the yardage listings and in the color wheel on the back cover. Use the color wheel to match fabrics to those from which the quilts were made.

Quilt diagrams or row diagrams are given where they might be helpful. These show the placement of blocks in the quilt, with each block labeled with its letter.

✱ The Rainbow Collection fabrics are available by the yard, and they are often presented as packets of ¼-yard pieces of each fabric, as well. Many of the projects in the book can be made from a single packet. For other projects, a packet will provide a good start. Additional yardage can be purchased in whichever colors are needed to complete the quilt.

Often, packets are made from "fat quarters." These are the equivalent of a quarter-yard, but they are 18"x 22" rather than 9" x 44" pieces. Occasionally where the yardage listing calls for ⅜ yard or even ½ yard, a fat quarter will suffice. For this reason, an asterisk has been used to indicate fabrics for which a fat quarter will suffice to cut the necessary patches.

All 48 colors of The Rainbow Collection are available at your local quilt shop, or you can send $2.00 for swatches to Quilts & Other Comforts, Box 394, Wheatridge, Colorado 80034-0394.

Quiltmaking Basics

MAKING TEMPLATES

Carefully trace pattern pieces directly onto clear template plastic, or trace on paper and glue to sandpaper, plastic, or cardboard. Cut out accurately to make template. See specific instructions for the sewing method of your choice to determine whether to trace seam lines or cutting lines when making templates.

Make a sample block to test the accuracy of your templates before cutting out the whole quilt.

PREPARATION

Always wash and iron fabrics before cutting them into patches. Rinse dark colors separately.

HAND PIECING

Patches for hand piecing require precisely marked seam lines, but marked cutting lines are optional. Most hand piecers prefer a template that does not include a seam allowance.

To mark the patches, place the template *face down* on wrong side of fabric and draw around it accurately with a pencil. Leave just enough space between patches to add ¼" seam allowances when cutting.

After marking the patches, cut outward from the seam line about ¼", measuring the distance by eye. The pieces will be joined right sides together, so the marked seam line on the wrong side of the fabric is visible on both sides of the patchwork when sewing. Sew the seam right through the penciled lines, so your patchwork will fit perfectly. Join the patches with a short running stitch, using a single thread. Begin and end each seam at seam line (not at edge of fabric) with two or three backstitches to secure seam.

MACHINE PIECING

Many machine patchworkers prefer to include the seam allowances in the template and mark the cutting line instead of the sewing line. When sewing patches together on the machine, align the cut edges with the edge of the presser foot if it is ¼" wide. If not, place a piece of masking tape on the throat plate of the machine ¼" away from the needle to guide you in making precise ¼" seams. Sew all the way to the cut edge unless you are inserting a patch into an angle.

HAND APPLIQUÉ

Templates for hand appliqué do not include turn-under allowances. To mark patches for hand appliqué, place template *face up* on right side of fabric; draw around it lightly with a pencil. Leave room for ³⁄₁₆" turn-under allowance around each patch.

Turn under ³⁄₁₆" allowance on each appliqué, and baste in place. (Do not turn under edges that will be tucked under other appliqués.) Clip into the turn-under allowance as needed for smooth curves.

Lay background block over printed pattern, matching centers, to see placement for appliqués. Pin appliqués into position.

Appliqué with a blind stitch in a thread color that matches the patch, not the background.

PRESSING

Press all seams to one side (not open), usually toward the darker fabric.

ADDING MITERED BORDERS

Center a border strip on each side of the quilt top to extend equally at each end. Pin, baste, and sew strips in ¼" seams, beginning and ending the seam at the seam line, not at outer edge of fabric. At one corner (on wrong side), smooth one border over an adjacent one and draw a diagonal line from inner seam line to the point where outer edges of two borders cross. Reverse the two borders (bottom one is now on top), and again draw a diagonal line from inner seam line to point where outer edges cross. Match the two pencil lines (fabrics right sides together), and sew through them. Cut away excess, and press seam to one side. Repeat at other three corners of quilt.

MARKING FOR QUILTING

Place quilting pattern under quilt top. Trace design on quilt top, marking very lightly with a hard lead pencil, a chalk pencil, or water soluble marker.

Outline quilting (¼" from seam around patches) or quilting "in the ditch" (right next to the seam on the side without the seam allowances) can be done "by eye." Other straight lines may also be "marked" as you quilt by using a piece of masking tape that is pulled away after a line is quilted along its edge.

LINING

Make a quilt lining about 2" larger on each side than the quilt top. Place lining, wrong side up, on a flat surface. Spread the quilt batt over the lining, keeping both smooth and even. Then place the quilt top, right side up, on top of the batting. Pin the three layers as necessary to hold them together while basting. Beginning in the center, baste all layers together in an "X," then in rows four to six inches apart. Also baste around edges.

QUILTING

Some quilters use a large frame; others use a hoop; and some use neither. Quilting is done in a short running stitch with a single strand of thread that goes through all three layers. Use a short needle (8 or 9 between) with about 18" of thread. Make a small knot in the thread, and take a first long stitch (about 1") through top and batting only, coming up where the quilting will begin. Tug on the thread to pull the knotted end between the layers. Take straight, even stitches that are the same size on the top and bottom sides of the quilt. For tiny stitches, push the needle with a thimble on your middle finger, and guide the fabric in front of the needle with the thumb of your hand above the quilt and thumb and index finger of your hand below the quilt. To end a line of quilting, take a tiny backstitch, and then make another inch-long stitch through the top and batting only. Clip thread at surface of quilt.

BINDING AND FINISHING

Trim quilt batt and lining even with quilt top. Leaving about 2" extra at each end, place a 1½" binding strip on one edge of quilt top, right sides together. Sew through all layers (binding, quilt top, batting, lining) with a ¼" seam, beginning and ending at seam line. Repeat for other three sides of quilt. Fold binding to the back, tucking under ¼", and blindstitch it down along seam line. At corners, trim, tuck in ends, and stitch.

Rainbow Log Cabin

Quick and easy are the bywords for this appealing quilt. If you like speed techniques, use a rotary cutter to cut pattern pieces several layers at a time. Or cut strips 1¾" wide and trim them to the proper length as you sew them. The quilt is shown in color on page 19.

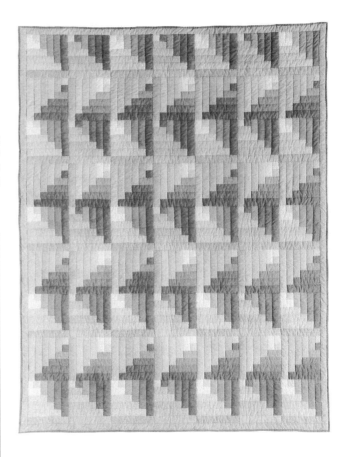

Rainbow Log Cabin: Lap Size

Block Size: 7½"	Fabric #15.......... ½ yd.
Quilt Size: 55" x 70"	31 F
Fabric #1 .... ¼ yd.*	Fabric #16.......... ½ yd.
32 B	31 E
Fabric #2 .... ⅛ yd.*	Fabric #17 .... 2 yds.
32 A	2 borders 1¾" x 70",
Fabric #3 .... ⅛ yd.*	2 borders 1¾" x 57½",
32 A	32 F
Fabric #5 .... ⅛ yd.*	Fabric #18.......... ⅞ yd.
31 A	binding 1½" x 7½ yds.,
Fabric #7 .... ¼ yd.*	32 E
31 B	Fabric #19.......... ½ yd.
Fabric #8 .... ⅛ yd.*	32 E
31 A	Fabric #20 .... ⅜ yd.*
Fabric #9 .... ¼ yd.*	32 D
31 C	Fabric #21......... ⅜ yd.*
Fabric #10 .... ¼ yd.*	32 D
31 B	Fabric #22 .... ¼ yd.*
Fabric #11 .... ⅜ yd.*	32 C
31 D	Fabric #23 .... ¼ yd.*
Fabric #12......... ¼ yd.*	32 C
31 C	Fabric #24 .... ¼ yd.*
Fabric #13.......... ½ yd.	32 B
31 E	Lining .... 3⅜ yds.
Fabric #14......... ⅜ yd.*	Batting .... 59" x 74"
31 D	*See page 4.

1. Match fabric numbers to numbered colors shown on back cover of book. Referring to diagrams, make 32 Y and 31 Z blocks.

2. See row diagrams. Join Y and Z blocks as shown to make five Row 1's and four Row 2's. Join rows, alternating types.

3. Add long borders to sides of quilt; trim ends. Add short borders to top and bottom; trim.

4. Quilt "in the ditch" around patches. Bind to finish.

Block Piecing

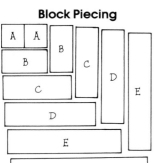
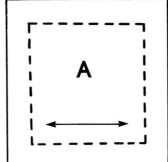

Rainbow Log Cabin: Bed Size

Block Size: 7½"	Fabric #15.......... ¾ yd.
Quilt Size: 85" x 100"	71 F
Fabric #1 .... ⅜ yd.	Fabric #16.......... ⅝ yd.
72 B	71 E
Fabric #2 .... ¼ yd.*	Fabric #17 .... 3 yds.
72 A	2 borders 1¾" x 100",
Fabric #3 .... ¼ yd.*	2 borders 1¾" x 87½",
72 A	72 F
Fabric #5 .... ¼ yd.*	Fabric #18....... 1¼ yds.
71 A	binding 1½" x 10¾
Fabric #7 .... ⅜ yd.	yds., 72 E
71 B	Fabric #19.......... ⅝ yd.
Fabric #8 .... ¼ yd.*	72 E
71 A	Fabric #20 .... ½ yd.
Fabric #9 .... ⅜ yd.	72 D
71 C	Fabric #21......... ½ yd.
Fabric #10 .... ⅜ yd.	72 D
71 B	Fabric #22 .... ⅜ yd.
Fabric #11 .... ½ yd.	72 C
71 D	Fabric #23 .... ⅜ yd.
Fabric #12......... ⅜ yd.	72 C
71 C	Fabric #24 .... ⅜ yd.
Fabric #13.......... ⅝ yd.	72 B
71 E	Lining .... 7⅝ yds.
Fabric #14......... ½ yd.	Batting .... 89" x 104"
71 D	*See page 4.

Match fabric numbers to numbered colors shown on back cover of book. Referring to diagrams, make 72 Y and 71 Z blocks. Turning blocks as shown in the photograph of the lap-size quilt, join six Y blocks alternately with five Z blocks to make a row. Make seven rows like this. Join six Z blocks alternately with five Y blocks to make a row. Make six rows like this. Join rows, alternating types. Finish quilt as described in steps 3-4 above.

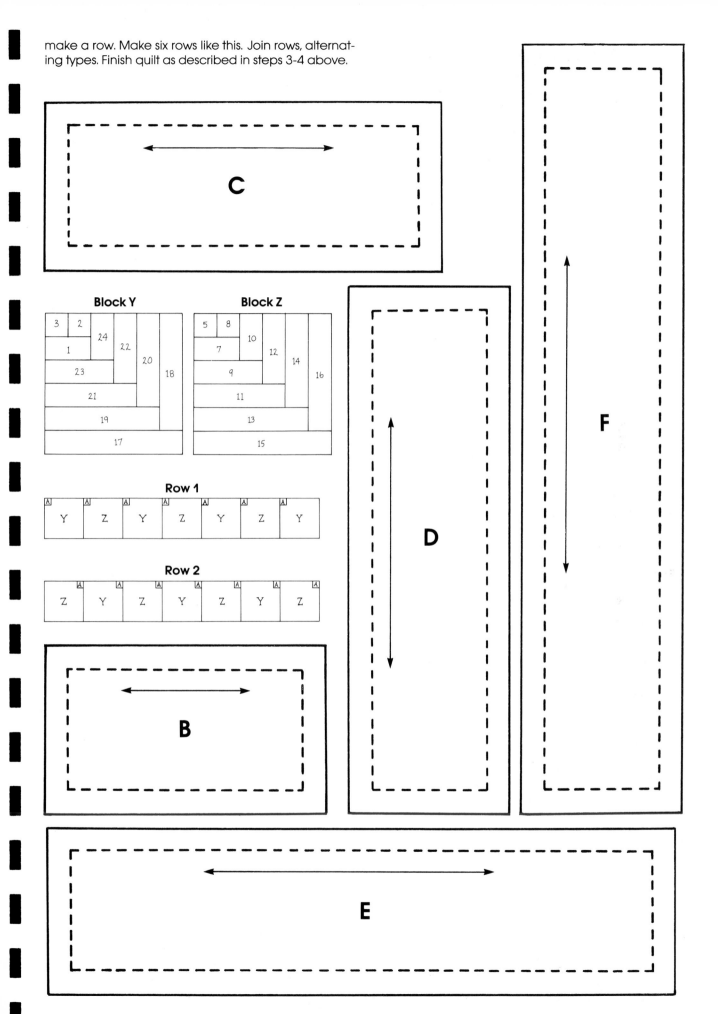

C

Block Y

3	2		
1	24	22	
23		20	18
21			
19			
17			

Block Z

5	8		
7	10	12	14
9			16
11			
13			
15			

Row 1

| A | A | A | A | A | A | A |
| Y | Z | Y | Z | Y | Z | Y |

Row 2

| A | A | A | A | A | A | A |
| Z | Y | Z | Y | Z | Y | Z |

B

D

F

E

Happily Ever After

If you've always admired the lovely Double Wedding Ring pattern but have hesitated to make it, here's the pattern you've been waiting for. This new variation is simplified—having about half the number of pieces of a traditional Wedding Ring. Instructions are given for a bed-size quilt and a quick wall quilt, both complete with a specially designed quilting pattern. The color photo is on page 20.

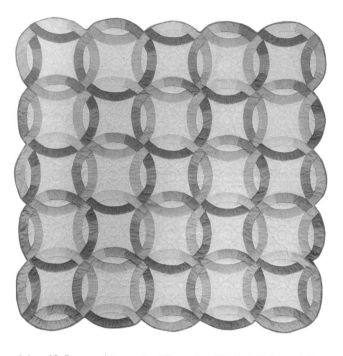

Happily Ever After: Wall Size

Block Size: 13⅝"	Fabric #14....... ⅛ yd.*
Quilt Size: 51⅜" x 51⅜"	15 E
Fabric #1 .... ⅛ yd.*	Fabric #15....... ⅛ yd.*
15 E	15 D
Fabric #2 .... ⅛ yd.*	Fabric #16....... ⅛ yd.*
15 E	15 D
Fabric #3 .... ⅛ yd.*	Fabric #17 .... ⅛ yd.*
15 D	15 C
Fabric #4 .... ⅛ yd.*	Fabric #18....... ⅛ yd.*
15 D	15 C
Fabric #5 .... ⅛ yd.*	Fabric #19....... ⅛ yd.*
15 C	15 E
Fabric #6 .... ⅛ yd.*	Fabric #20 ...... ⅛ yd.*
15 C	15 E
Fabric #7 .... ⅛ yd.*	Fabric #21....... ⅛ yd.*
15 E	15 D
Fabric #8 .... ⅛ yd.*	Fabric #22 ...... ⅛ yd.*
15 E	15 D
Fabric #9 .... ⅛ yd.*	Fabric #23 ...... ⅛ yd.*
15 D	15 C
Fabric #10......... ⅛ yd.*	Fabric #24 ...... ⅛ yd.*
15 D	15 C
Fabric #11 .... ⅛ yd.*	Cream.......... 1¾ yds.
15 C	25 A, 60 B
Fabric #12.......... ⅞ yd.	Lining .... 3¼ yds.
binding 1½" x 8½ yds.,	Batting.... 55½" x 55½"
15 C	
Fabric #13......... ⅛ yd.*	
15 E	*See page 4.

1. Match fabric numbers to numbered colors shown on back cover of book. Referring to unit diagrams and Fig. 1, join C-D-E. Match center of B to center of D, and stitch from center point to end of E. Leave other end free. Join C-D-E and stitch to other side of B, as shown in Fig. 2. Complete the seam that joins D and C to other side of B. Repeat to make 15 each of Units 1, 2, 3, and 4.

2. Join A patches with Units 1 and 2 to make three Row 1's and two Row 2's as shown in the diagram. Join rows, alternating types and inserting Units 3 and 4 into the curves as shown.

3. Mark and quilt the motif given in the A patches. Quilt "in the ditch" around all patches. Make bias binding, and attach, smoothing out the blunted parts of C patches around edges of quilt.

Row Diagram

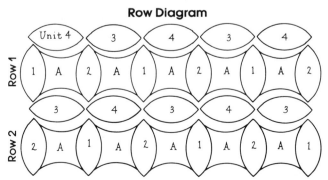

Happily Ever After: Bed Size

Block Size: 13⅝"	Fabric #14........ ⅜ yd.
Quilt Size: 89⅛" x 108"	54 E
Fabric #1 .... ⅜ yd.	Fabric #15........ ½ yd.
54 E	54 D
Fabric #2 .... ⅜ yd.	Fabric #16........ ½ yd.
54 E	54 D
Fabric #3 .... ½ yd.	Fabric #17 .... ½ yd.
54 D	54 C
Fabric #4 .... ½ yd.	Fabric #18........ ½ yd.
54 D	54 C
Fabric #5 .... ½ yd.	Fabric #19........ ⅜ yd.
54 C	55 E
Fabric #6 .... ½ yd.	Fabric #20 .... ⅜ yd.
54 C	55 E
Fabric #7 .... ⅜ yd.	Fabric #21........ ½ yd.
55 E	55 D
Fabric #8 .... ⅜ yd.	Fabric #22 .... ½ yd.
55 E	55 D
Fabric #9 .... ½ yd.	Fabric #23 .... ½ yd.
55 D	55 C
Fabric #10......... ½ yd.	Fabric #24 .... ½ yd.
55 D	55 C
Fabric #11 .... ½ yd.	Cream.......... 6⅜ yds.
55 C	99 A, 218 B
Fabric #12....... 1½ yds.	Lining .... 8 yds.
binding 1½" x 14 yds.,	Batting........ 93" x 112"
55 C	
Fabric #13.......... ⅜ yd.	
54 E	

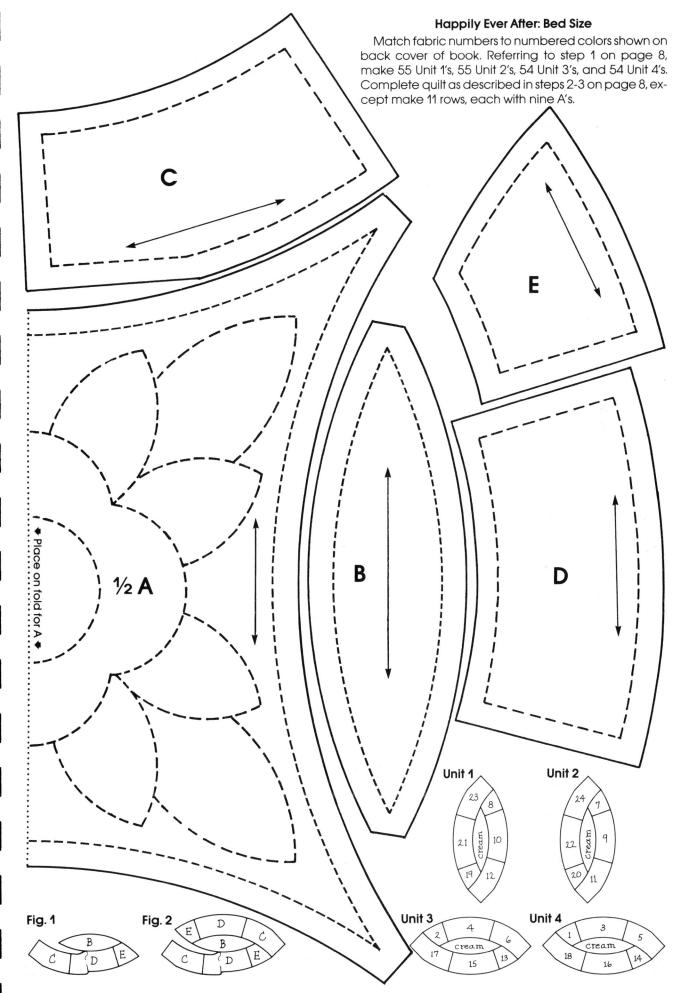

Happily Ever After: Bed Size
Match fabric numbers to numbered colors shown on back cover of book. Referring to step 1 on page 8, make 55 Unit 1's, 55 Unit 2's, 54 Unit 3's, and 54 Unit 4's. Complete quilt as described in steps 2-3 on page 8, except make 11 rows, each with nine A's.

C

E

½ A

◆ Place on fold for A ◆

B

D

Unit 1

23	8
21	cream	10
19	12

Unit 2

24	7
22	cream	9
20	11

Fig. 1

C B E
  C D E

Fig. 2

E D C
  C B E
  C D E

Unit 3

2	4	6
17	cream	13
15

Unit 4

1	3	5
18	cream	14
16

9

Crayon Box

Remember what fun a new box of crayons gave you as a child? Give that same joy to a favorite youngster by making a gift of this charming, but simple, quilt. The easy shapes are suitable for rotary cutting or scissor cutting through several layers, and the sewing is a breeze. The color photo is on page 20.

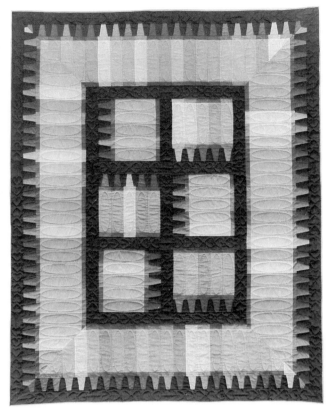

Block Size: 11¼"	**Fabric #15** .... ¼ yd.*
Quilt Size: 56¼" x 69¾"	11 A
Fabric #1 .... ¼ yd.*	**Fabric #16** .... ⅛ yd.*
10 A	20 B, 12 C
Fabric #2 .... ⅛ yd.*	**Fabric #17** .... ¼ yd.*
18 B, 11 C	10 A
Fabric #3 .... ¼ yd.*	**Fabric #18** .... ⅛ yd.*
11 A	18 B, 10 C
Fabric #4 .... ⅛ yd.*	**Fabric #19** .... ¼ yd.*
20 B, 12 C	11 A
Fabric #5 .... ¼ yd.*	**Fabric #20** .... ⅛ yd.*
10 A	20 B, 12 C
Fabric #6 .... ⅛ yd.*	**Fabric #21** .... ¼ yd.*
18 B, 10 C	10 A
Fabric #7 .... ¼ yd.*	**Fabric #22** .... ⅛ yd.*
11 A	18 B, 11 C
Fabric #8 .... ⅛ yd.*	**Fabric #23** .... ¼ yd.*
20 B, 12 C	11 A
Fabric #9 .... ¼ yd.*	**Fabric #24** .... ⅛ yd.*
10 A	20 B, 11 C
Fabric #10 .... ⅛ yd.*	**Dark Purple** ..... 2⅛ yds.
18 B, 11 C	2 borders 2¾" x 72¼",
Fabric #11 .... ¼ yd.*	2 borders 2¾" x 58¾",
11 A	2 borders 2¾" x 45¼",
Fabric #12 .... ⅛ yd.*	2 borders 2¾" x 31¾",
20 B, 11 C	2 sashes 2¾" x 25¼",
Fabric #13 .... ¾ yd.	132 C, 6 D, 6 Dr, 3 E
binding 1½" x 7½ yds.,	**Lining** .... 3½ yds.
10 A	**Batting** .... 60" x 74"
Fabric #14 .... ⅛ yd.*	
18 B, 11 C	*See page 4.

1. Match fabric numbers to numbered colors shown on back cover of book. Referring to diagrams, make six blocks, pairing colors 1 and 2, 3 and 4, 5 and 6, and so on. Color sequence of crayons in block is random.

2. Referring to quilt photograph and turning blocks as desired, sew a sash (E) between two blocks to make a row. Repeat to make three rows. Join rows with 25¼" sashes between them.

3. See Fig. 1. Arrange patches for 15 crayons in a row for top pieced border. To each end add patches for three crayons without the bottom B. Add a C to each end. Be sure to include the 24 dark purple C's between crayon tips. Join the C's in order to make a row. Similarly join B's, A's, and B's again to make three more rows. Join rows. Matching centers, sew 31¾" strip to inner edge and 58¾" strip to outer edge of pieced crayon strip. Sew to top of quilt, again matching centers. Repeat for bottom of quilt. Similarly, make a side border with 21 whole crayons plus partial crayons and dark purple C's as shown in Fig. 2. Add 45¼" strip to inner edge and 72¼" strip to outer edge of crayon strip, matching centers. Again matching centers, sew to side of quilt. Repeat for other side. Miter corners and trim excess.

4. Mark quilting motifs given in A and E patches. Mark motif from E patch in sashes and inner and outer borders. Motifs should align with blocks. Mark two motifs in each long sash and in each short inner border. Mark three motifs in each long inner border. Mark four motifs

Block Piecing

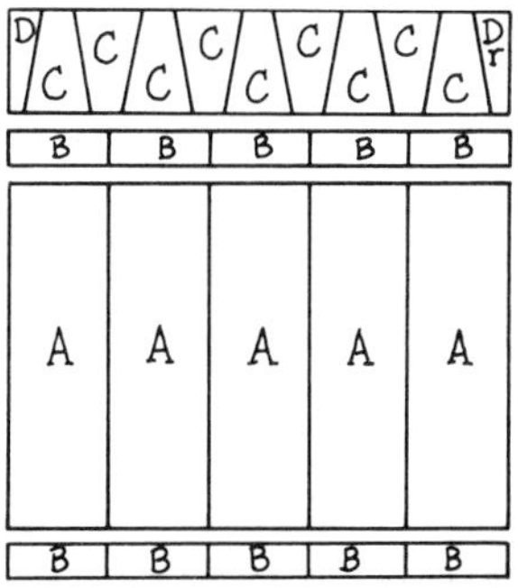

Crayon Coloring

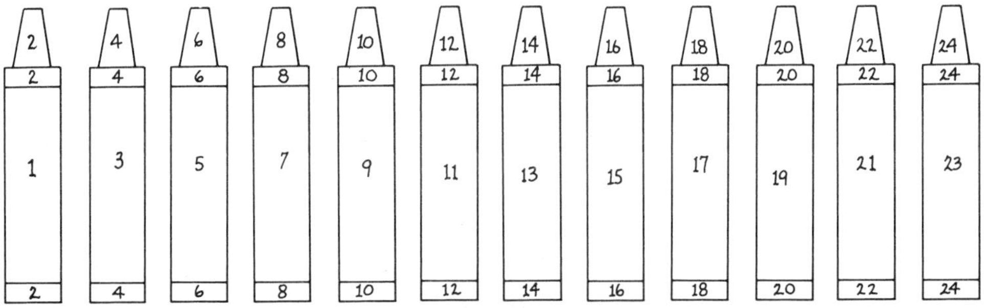

in each short outer border. Mark five motifs in each
long outer border. Quilt as marked. Quilt "in the ditch"
between patches. Quilt a 3¼"-long straight line to connect each pair of neighboring motifs in borders and
sashes. Bind to finish.

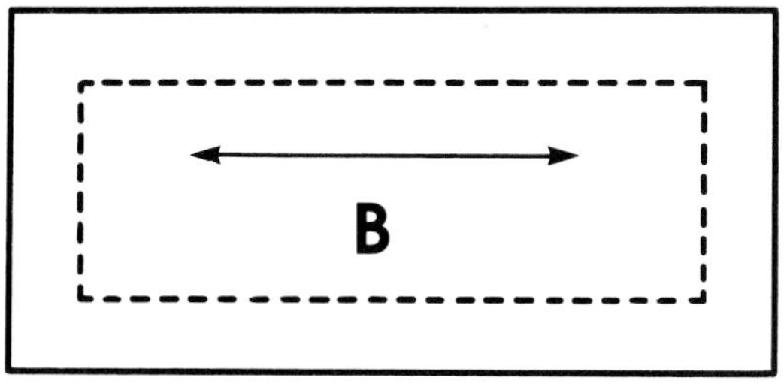

B

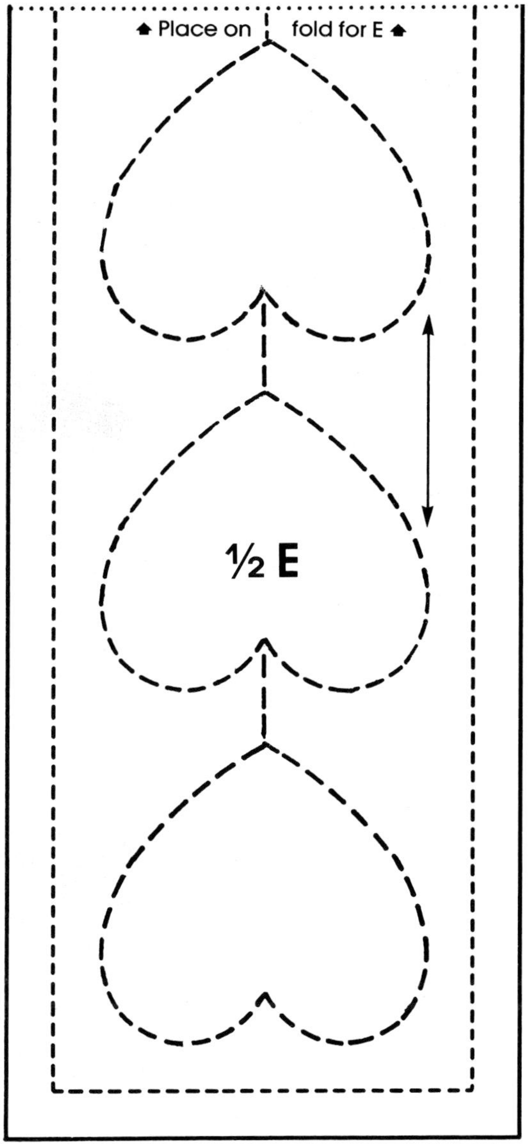

♠ Place on ┆ fold for E ♠

½ E

Fig. 1

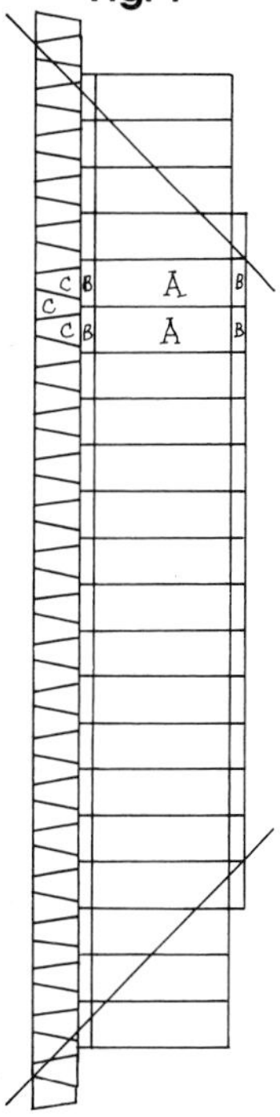

C B Ā B
C B Ā B

A

Fig. 2

C B Ā B
C B Ā B

D &
Dr

C

11

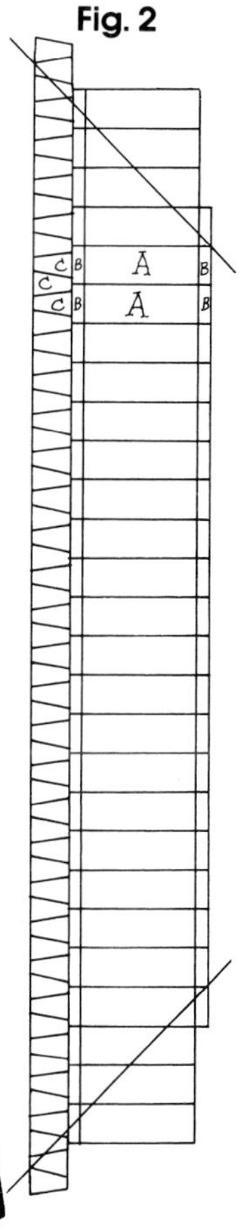

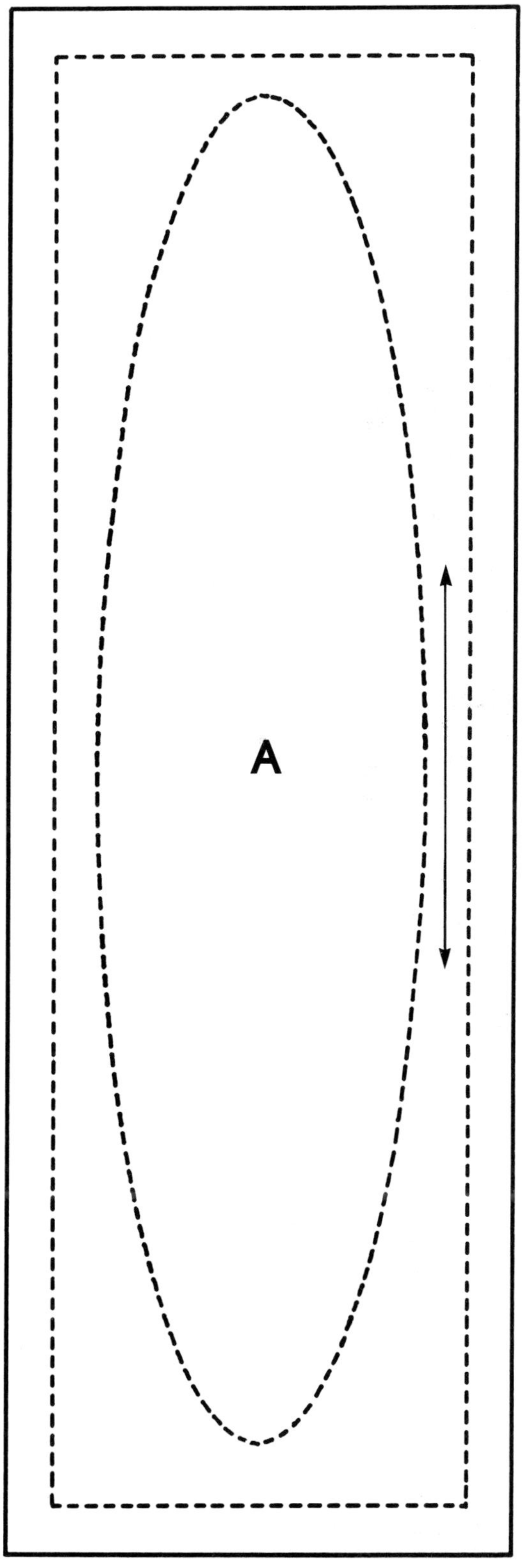

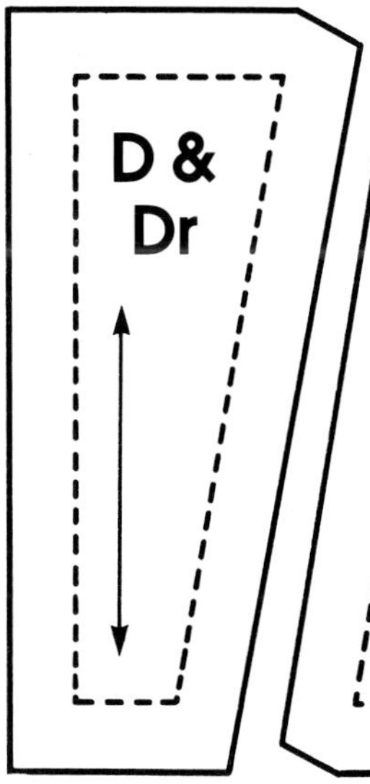

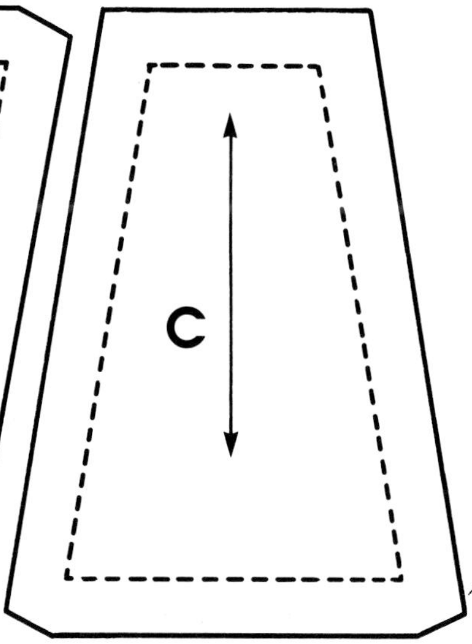

Pot O' Gold

This quilt is a real treasure—the pot of gold at the end of the rainbow. It's fascinating to look at but quick to make. Use rotary cutting, strip piecing, or any of your favorite speed techniques to piece the quilt in a jiffy. The quilt is shown in color on page 21.

Block Size: 10"	**Fabric #15** .... 1¼ yds.
Quilt Size: 76" x 96"	binding 1½" x 10⅛ yds.,
Fabric #1 .... 1¾ yds.	135 C
32 A, 128 B	**Fabric #17** .... ⅝ yd.
Fabric #4 .... ¾ yd.	119 C
133 C	**Fabric #19** .... ¾ yd.
Fabric #6 .... ⅝ yd.	134 C
116 C	**Fabric #21** .... ⅝ yd.
Fabric #8 .... ¾ yd.	119 C
132 C	**Fabric #23** .... ¾ yd.
Fabric #10 .... ⅝ yd.	135 C
116 C	**Lining** .... 5¾ yds.
Fabric #12 .... ¾ yd.	**Batting** .... 80" x 100"
133 C	
Fabric #13 .... 2⅞ yds.	
2 borders 2½" x 98½",	
2 borders 2½" x 78½"	

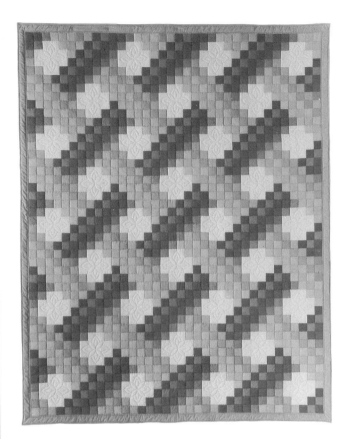

1. Match fabric numbers to numbered colors shown on back cover of book. Referring to diagrams, make 32 X blocks, 15 Y blocks, and 16 Z blocks.

2. Keeping blocks turned as shown in block diagrams, join blocks into nine rows as shown in quilt diagram. Join rows.

3. Referring to diagrams below and on next page, join squares to make bottom strip and right side strip. Sew these strips to bottom and right edge of quilt respectively.

4. Add borders, mitering corners and trimming excess from seam allowances.

5. With pencil, trace A patch surrounded by four B patches as shown in Fig. 1 below. (Leave off seam allowances.) These lines are for position only. With a black pen, trace the quilting motifs given in the A and B patches. Be careful to turn the motif in the B patches to complete the petals around the edges of A. Mark this complete motif over each of the 32 groups of A-B patches in the quilt. Quilt as marked. Quilt "in the ditch" between patches except along seams between A's and B's. Quilt ¼" from long seams of border. Bind to finish.

Fig. 1

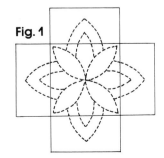

Quilt Diagram

X	Y	X	Y	X	Y	X
Z	X	Z	X	Z	X	Z
X	Y	X	Y	X	Y	X
Z	X	Z	X	Z	X	Z
X	Y	X	Y	X	Y	X
Z	X	Z	X	Z	X	Z
X	Y	X	Y	X	Y	X
Z	X	Z	X	Z	X	Z
X	Y	X	Y	X	Y	X

Bottom Strip

19	17	15	12	10	8	6	4	23	21	19	17	15	12	10	8	6	4	23	21	19	17	15	12	10	8	6	4	23	21	19	17	15	12	10

Block X

8	6	4	23	21
6	4	1		23
4		1	1	1
15	1			
17	15	1		12

Block X Piecing

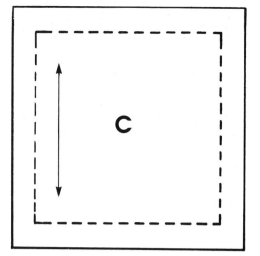

C	C	C	C	C
C	C	B		C
C		B	A	B
C				
C	C	B		C

C

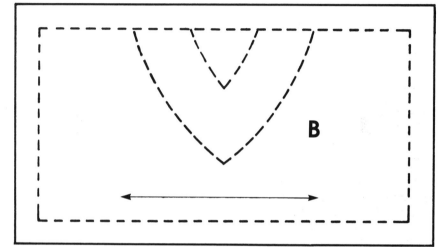

B

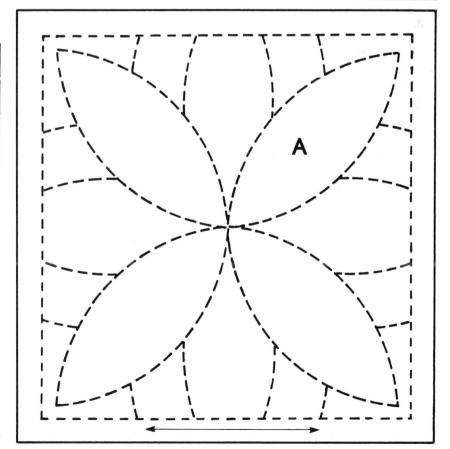

A

Right Side Strip

19
21
23
12
10
8
6
4
15
17
19
21
23
12
10
8
6
4
15
17
19
21
23
12
10
8
6
4
15
17
19
21
23
12
10
8
6
4
15
17
19
21
23
12
10
8

Block Y

19	17	15	12	10
21	19	12	10	8
23	12	10	8	6
12	10	8	6	4
10	8	6	4	19

Blocks Y & Z Piecing

C	C	C	C	C
C	C	C	C	C
C	C	C	C	C
C	C	C	C	C
C	C	C	C	C
C	C	C	C	C

Block Z

19	17	15	12	10
21	19	17	15	8
23	21	19	17	15
12	23	21	19	17
10	8	23	21	19

Cotton Candy

This quilt is as sweet as cotton candy and as colorful and lively as a carnival. Can't you just see the Ferris wheels spinning? Don't be put off by the hexagon-shaped blocks. There's nothing to set in, as you can see from the diagrams. This quilt was cut out and machine pieced in just 8½ hours. Even the bed-size quilt would be refreshingly quick to make. The Cotton Candy quilt is shown in color on page 22.

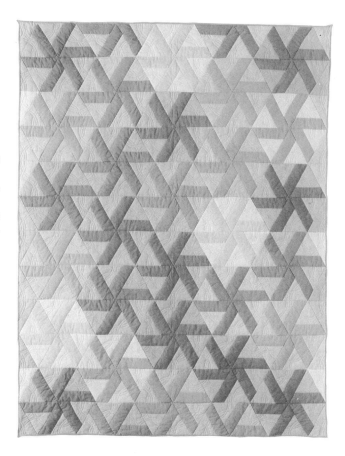

Cotton Candy: Nap Size

Quilt Size: 46" x 60"	Fabric #14......... ¼ yd.*
Fabric #1 .... ¼ yd.*	18 B
18 A, 1 C, 1 Cr	Fabric #15......... ¼ yd.*
Fabric #2 .... ¼ yd.*	18 A, 1 C, 1 Cr
18 B	Fabric #16......... ¼ yd.*
Fabric #3 .... ¼ yd.*	18 B
12 A, 1 C, 1 Cr	Fabric #17 .... ¼ yd.*
Fabric #4 .... ¼ yd.*	12 A, 1 C, 1 Cr
12 B	Fabric #18......... ¼ yd.*
Fabric #5 .... ¼ yd.*	12 B
12 A, 1 C, 1 Cr	Fabric #19......... ¼ yd.*
Fabric #6 .... ¼ yd.*	12 A, 1 C, 1 Cr
12 B	Fabric #20 .... ¼ yd.*
Fabric #7 .... ¼ yd.*	12 B
18 A, 1 C, 1 Cr	Fabric #21......... ¼ yd.*
Fabric #8 .... ¼ yd.*	12 A, 1 C, 1 Cr
18 B	Fabric #22 .... ¼ yd.*
Fabric #9 .... ¼ yd.*	12 B
18 A, 1 C, 1 Cr	Fabric #23 .... ¼ yd.*
Fabric #10...,....... 1 yd.	18 A, 1 C, 1 Cr
binding 1½" x 6½ yds.,	Fabric #24 .... ¼ yd.*
18 B	18 B
Fabric #11 .... ¼ yd.*	Lining .... 3 yds.
12 A, 1 C, 1 Cr	Batting........... 50" x 64"
Fabric #12......... ¼ yd.*	
12 B	
Fabric #13......... ¼ yd.*	
18 A, 1 C, 1 Cr	*See page 4.

1. Match fabric numbers to numbered colors shown on back cover of book. Referring to diagram, make 180 Unit 1's, pairing fabrics #1-2, 3-4, 5-6, 7-8, and so on. Join 3 matching Unit 1's to make a Unit 2. Make 60 Unit 2's.

2. Referring to photograph and row diagram, arrange the Unit 2's, five to a row, turning every other unit upside down. Be careful to arrange matching Unit 2's in pairs to complete hexagons. When you are pleased with the balance and arrangement of the colors, separate the units into 12 rows as shown in the row diagram. (Every other row will be upside down.) Join units into rows. Sew a C and a Cr to the ends of each row. Join rows.

3. Mark quilting given in the A, C, and Cr patches. Quilt as marked, and quilt "in the ditch" around the patches. Bind to finish.

Cotton Candy: Bed Size

Quilt Size: 80½" x 100"	Fabric #13.......... ½ yd.
Fabric #1 .... ½ yd.	42 A
42 A	Fabric #14.......... ⅝ yd.
Fabric #2 .... ⅝ yd.	42 B
42 B	Fabric #15.......... ½ yd.
Fabric #3 .... ½ yd.	48 A
48 A	Fabric #16.......... ⅝ yd.
Fabric #4 .... ⅝ yd.	48 B
48 B	Fabric #17 .... ½ yd.
Fabric #5 .... ½ yd.	42 A
42 A	Fabric #18.......... ⅝ yd.
Fabric #6 .... ⅝ yd.	42 B
42 B	Fabric #19.......... ½ yd.
Fabric #7 .... ½ yd.	48 A
48 A	Fabric #20 .... ⅝ yd.
Fabric #8 .... 1⅜ yds.	48 B
binding 1½" x 11 yds.,	Fabric #21.......... ½ yd.
48 B	42 A
Fabric #9 .... ½ yd.	Fabric #22 .... ⅝ yd.
42 A	42 B
Fabric #10.......... ⅝ yd.	Fabric #23 .... ½ yd.
42 B	48 A
Fabric #11 .... ½ yd.	Fabric #24 .... ⅝ yd.
48 A	48 B
Fabric #12.......... ⅝ yd.	Lining .... 7⅜ yds.
48 B	Batting....... 84½" x 104"

Match fabric numbers to numbered colors shown on back cover of book. Referring to diagram, make 540 Unit 1's, coordinating fabrics as described in step 1 at left. Join these in sets of three matching units to make 180 Unit 2's. Complete quilt as described in steps 2-3 at left, except make 20 rows of nine units each.

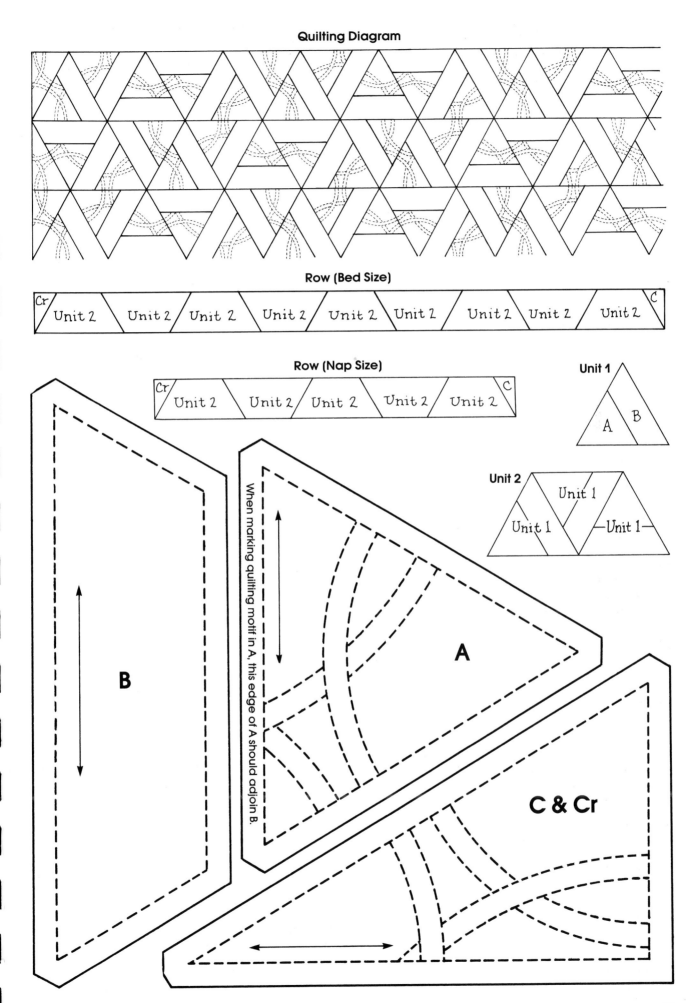

Quilting Diagram

Row (Bed Size)

| Cr | Unit 2 | Unit 2 | Unit 2 | Unit 2 | Unit 2 | Unit 2 | Unit 2 | Unit 2 | Unit 2 | C |

Row (Nap Size)

| Cr | Unit 2 | Unit 2 | Unit 2 | Unit 2 | Unit 2 | C |

Unit 1

A   B

Unit 2

Unit 1   Unit 1   Unit 1

B

When marking quilting motif in A, this edge of A should adjoin B.

A

C & Cr

Hearts Awhirl

Nostalgic images of fans, hearts, and flowers combine in this romantic confection. The effect is truly special, although the quilt can be made quite quickly on account of its small size. Why not make it as a wedding or anniversary gift or a memorable valentine? A color picture is on page 22.

Block Sizes: 10″, 20 ″	**Fabric #16** .... ⅛ yd.*
Quilt Size: 53″ x 53″	4 A, 4 B, 4 I
Fabric #2 .... ⅛ yd.*	**Fabric #17** .... 1⅜ yds.
4 A, 4 B	4 borders 3″ x 47½″,
Fabric #4 .... ⅜ yd.*	8 E
4 A, 4 B, 8 F, 8 H	**Fabric #18** .... 1⅝ yds.
Fabric #6 .... ⅜ yd.*	4 borders 4½″ x 55½″,
8 bias strips ¾″ x 9½″,	4 A, 4 B, 16 E
4 A, 4 B, 8 G	**Fabric #20** .... ⅛ yd.*
Fabric #8 .... ⅛ yd.*	4 A, 4 B
4 A, 4 B	**Fabric #22** .... ⅛ yd.*
Fabric #10 .... ⅛ yd.*	4 A, 4 B
4 A, 4 B	**Fabric #24** .... ⅛ yd.*
Fabric #11 .... ⅝ yd.	4 A, 4 B
1 J	**Plum Solid** .... ¾ yd.
Fabric #12 .... ⅛ yd.*	binding 1½″ x 6½ yds.,
4 A, 4 B	8 C
Fabric #13 .... ⅜ yd.	**Lining** .... 3¼ yds.
8 D	**Batting** .... 57″ x 57″
Fabric #14 .... ⅛ yd.*	
4 A, 4 B	
Fabric #15 .... ⅜ yd.	
4 K	*See page 4.

1. Match fabric numbers to numbered colors shown on back cover of book. Join four I patches to make a star; turn under raw edges and position in center of J; blindstitch.

2. Turn under edges of appliqués ³⁄₁₆″ and baste. Make bias strips for stems as follows: fold bias stripping in half lengthwise with wrong sides together. Stitch in a ⅛″ seam. Press strip to conceal seam and seam allowance on underside as shown in Fig. 1 on page 17.

3. Referring to W and Z diagrams, position background square over pattern to see placement for appliqués. Pin patches in position, starting with bias stems, then proceeding in alphabetical order. Blindstitch in thread to match each patch. Trim away background fabric from behind each patch. Make one W block and four Z blocks.

4. Referring to diagrams, make four X blocks and four Y blocks. Appliqué an E centered in each C patch.

5. Join X and Y blocks with X on the left, as shown. Join these with W and Z blocks, as shown in the quilt diagram on page 17, to make three rows. Join rows.

6. Join wide and narrow border strips, matching centers. Sew to sides of quilt with narrow strip touching blocks, again matching centers. Miter corners, trimming excess from seam allowances.

7. See Figs. 2 and 3 on page 18. Mark quilting motif given in D patches. Use the part of this motif extending between the dots for quilting the outer borders. Find

Block W

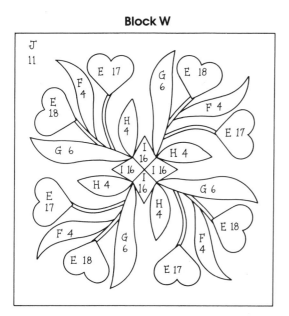

Block X

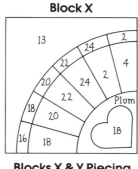

Block Y

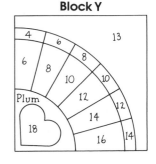

Blocks X & Y Piecing

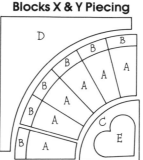

Block Z

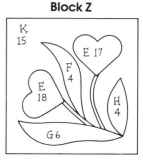

B

border center by folding border in half crosswise. Mark the first border motif with the center line of the motif over the center of the border. The two dots should be ¾" from the seam line joining wide and narrow borders. Mark seven motifs in each border, matching dots of one motif with dots of the next. Mark one ribbon tail and two reversed ribbon tails over each miter at corners. Quilt as marked. Quilt "in the ditch" around all patches. Quilt ¼" from long seam lines of narrow, inner border. Bind to finish.

Fig. 1

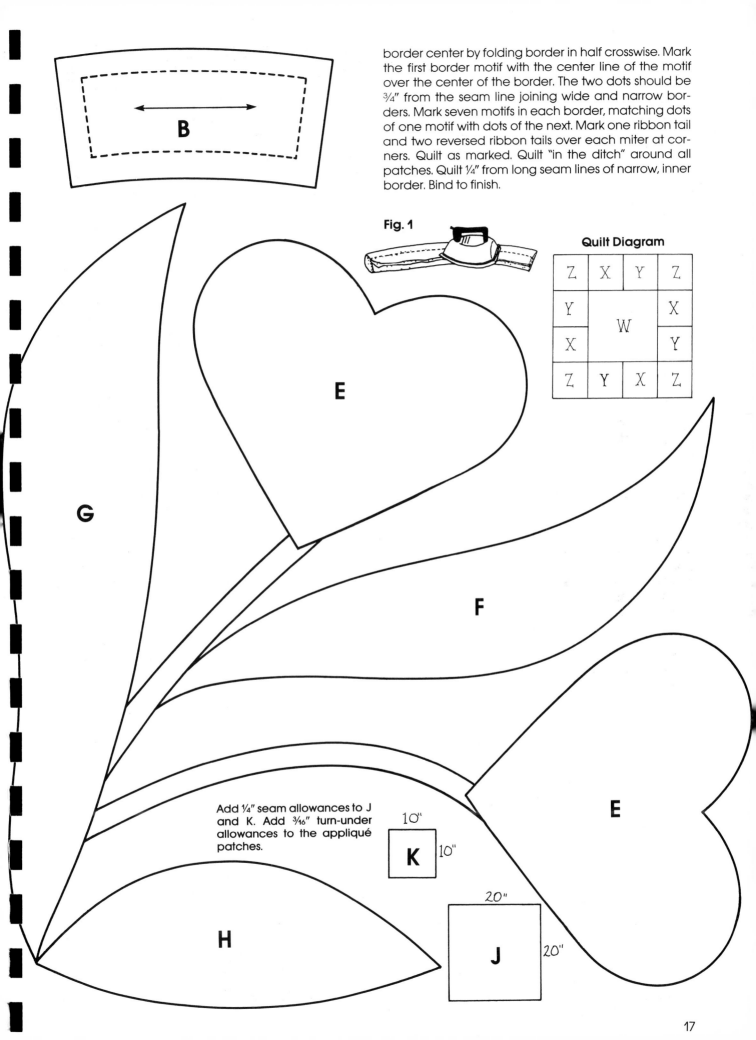

Quilt Diagram

Z	X	Y	Z
Y			X
X	W		Y
Z	Y	X	Z

E

G

F

E

Add ¼" seam allowances to J and K. Add ³⁄₁₆" turn-under allowances to the appliqué patches.

10"

K   10"

20"

J   20"

H

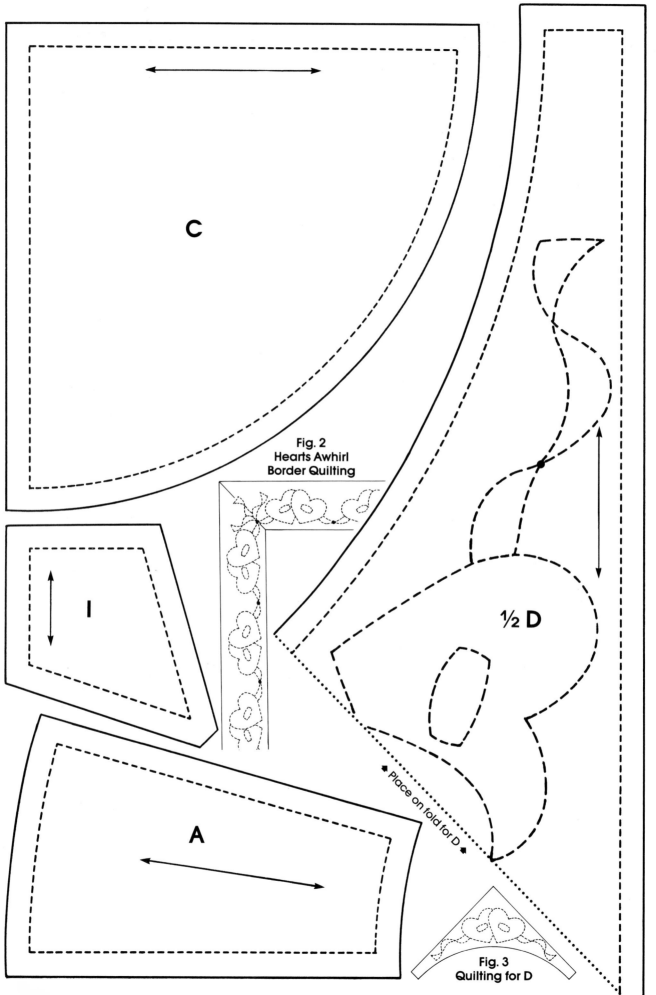

C

Fig. 2
Hearts Awhirl
Border Quilting

I

½ D

A

Place on fold for D

Fig. 3
Quilting for D

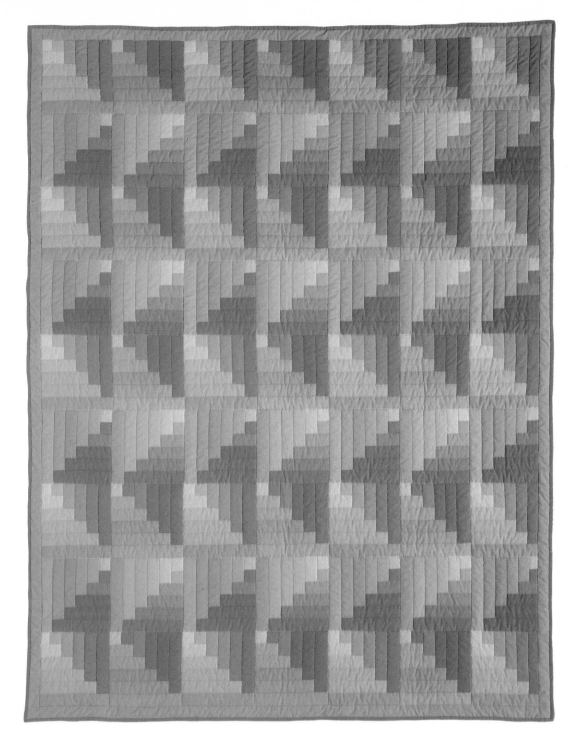

Rainbow Log Cabin, 55" x 70", 1987. Pieced by Doxa Brune; quilted by Barbara Zygiel. Based on a traditional block; adapted for rainbow colors by the author. The Log Cabin is a perennial favorite; it looks like what a quilt should be: full of heart and a simple grace, with one foot in the past and an eye on the future. Rainbow Log Cabin calls up all the traditional images and the warmth of a rich heritage, and yet it looks completely at home today. Find the pattern on page 6.

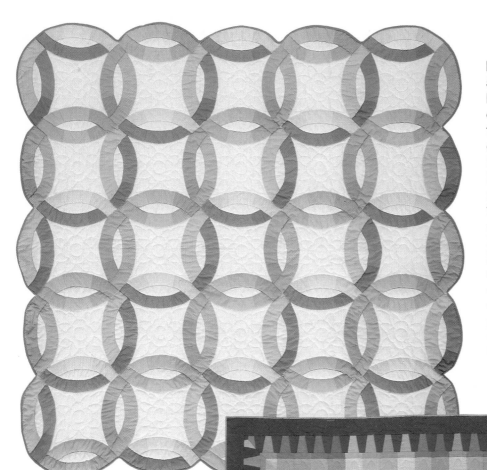

Happily Ever After, 51⅜″ x 51⅜″, 1987. Made by Barbaralee Pressler from a design by the author. A traditional Double Wedding Ring was simplified a little and adapted for rainbow colors. Light and medium color wheels interlock in this attractive design. In the pastel rainbow colors shown, the quilt has an airy look. For a richer, more substantial look, choose darker rainbow colors with a coordinated pastel background. The pattern for this quilt and a bed-size version begin on page 8.

Crayon Box, 56¼″ x 69¾″, 1987. Made by Jackie Madison. Designed by the author. Pieced picture quilts seem to be the quilts of the '80s, and this is one of the easiest pieced picture patterns ever devised. "Crayons" are arranged randomly for a casual, colorful look. Additional colors could easily be incorporated into the plan. See the pattern and instructions starting on page 10.

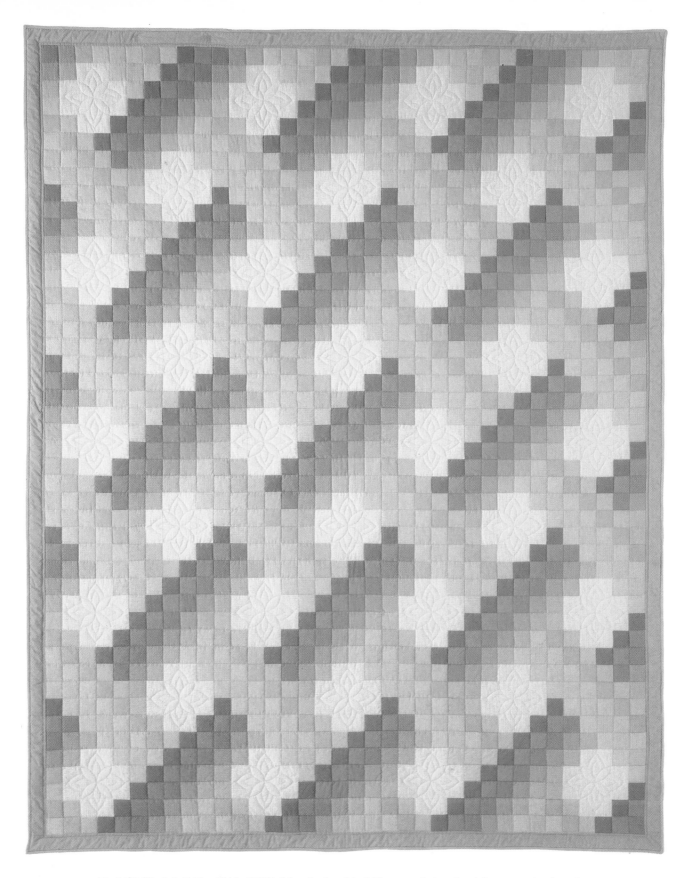

Pot O' Gold, 76" x 96", 1987. Made by Nell Torrez. Adapted from a design by Marilyn Martinez. Glorious rainbows stair-step and weave across the surface of this quilt, reminiscent of an Irish Chain. The colors interact delightfully, hiding the fact that this is really a very simple quilt. See the pattern and instructions on page 12.

Hearts Awhirl, 53" x 53", 1987. Made by Shirley Wegert. Designed by the author. Familiar quilt motifs of fans, hearts, and flowers make an especially pretty combination here. The look is sweet and gentle. For an equally pretty quilt with more striking contrast, choose darker rainbow shades for the appliqués. The pattern begins on page 16.

Cotton Candy, 46" x 60", 1987. Pieced by Marla Stefanelli; quilted by Mina Slade. Adapted for rainbow colors by the author. The traditional Whirling Hexagons pattern provided the idea for this scrumptious quilt. Unlike most hexagon quilts, this one can be sewn entirely in straight rows without setting in any patches. Rainbow colors in darker shades could be added for a touch of contrast if desired. Patterns and instructions for this quilt and a bed-size version are on page 14.

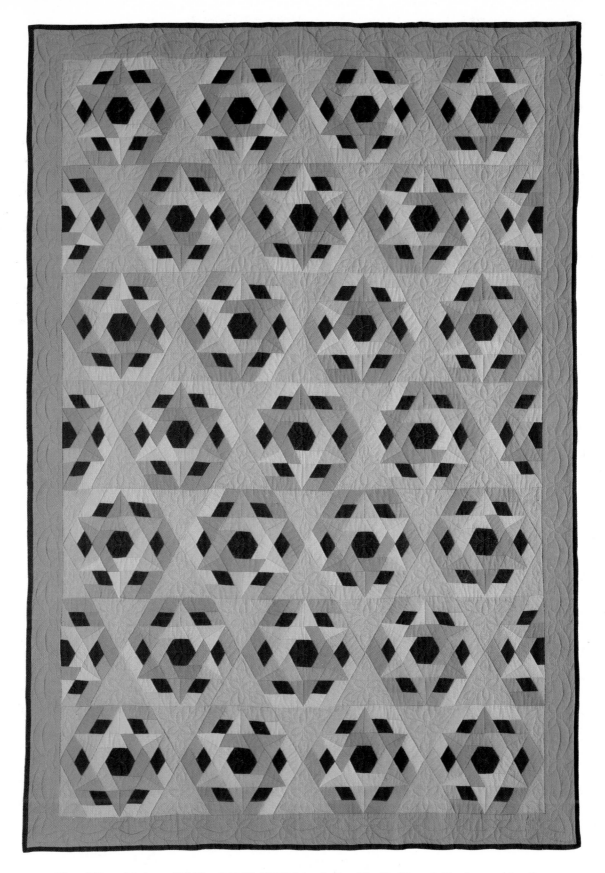

The Silver Lining, 57½" x 84¾", 1987. Made by Phyllis Street. Designed by the author. In the soft rainbow colors shown or in darker, moody ones, this quilt would have the same irresistible appeal. It's the combination of color wheels, stars, interlocked rings, and folded-paper dimensionality that makes this quilt a delight. The pattern begins on page 27.

Twilight Rainbow, 72" x 82½", 1987. Pieced by Reni Dieball; quilted by Wendy Dodge. Based on a traditional 54-40 or Fight block and adapted for rainbow colors by the author. Orderly color progressions in both the blocks and border make this quilt a standout. For a more subdued effect, light rainbow colors could be substituted for the white, and the stars and squares could be darker rainbow shades. The pattern and instructions are on page 30.

Rainbow Ribbon Twist, 92⅜" x 103", 1987. Pieced by Jonna Castle; quilted by Margaret Waltz. Adapted from a design by Audrey Humphrey. Big, strip-pieced patches make this quilt as graphically striking as it is easy. Curved quilting in a Gordian knot motif softens the angles and adds texture. The pattern begins on page 32.

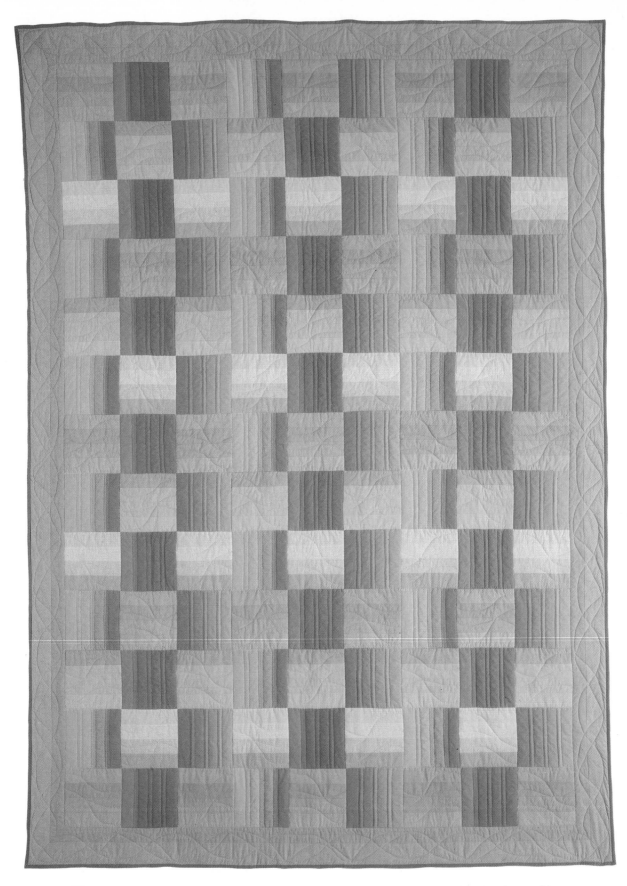

Rainbow Weave, 71¾" x 99¾", 1987. Made by Daphne Wells. Designed by the author. A traditional Basket Weave pattern looks altogether different in softly blended rainbow colors. The random curves quilted in the light patches soften the geometric shapes and add a fluid grace. For a similar quilt with a more rugged and less sweet look, choose darker rainbow colors. Pattern and instructions are on page 34.

The Silver Lining

There's nothing tricky to cloud your enjoyment of making this attractive quilt. It's the rainbow without the rain, the silver lining all by itself. Simply follow the diagrams and you'll have a quilt to be proud of. See the quilt in color on page 23.

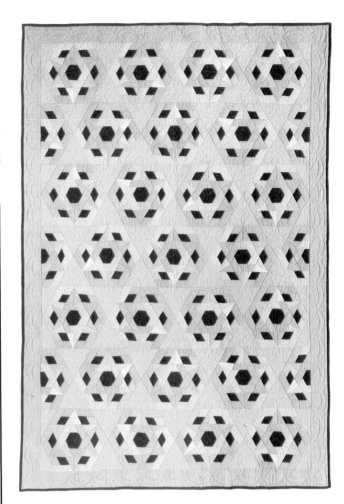

Block Size: 11¼"	**Fabric #16**.......... ¾ yd.
Quilt Size: 57½" x 84¾"	27 B, 28 Cr, 28 D, 28 E,
Fabric #2 .... ⅛ yd.*	1 F, 1 G
28 C	**Fabric #18**......... ⅛ yd.*
Fabric #4 .... ¾ yd.	28 C
27 B, 28 Cr, 28 D, 28 E,	**Fabric #20** .... ¾ yd.
1 F, 1 G	27 B, 28 Cr, 28 D, 28 E,
Fabric #6 .... ⅛ yd.*	1 F, 1 G
28 C	**Fabric #22** .... ⅛ yd.*
Fabric #8 .... 2½ yds.	28 C
2 borders 3½" x 87¼",	**Fabric #24** .... ¾ yd.
2 borders 3½" x 60",	27 B, 28 Cr, 28 D, 28 E,
27 B, 28 Cr, 28 D, 28 E,	1 F, 1 G
1 F, 1 G	**Dk. Gray** .... 1⅝ yds.
Fabric #10 .... ⅛ yd.*	binding 1½" x 8½ yds.,
28 C	25 A, 168 D, 6 H
Fabric #12 .... ¾ yd.	**Lt. Gray** .... 1⅜ yds.
27 B, 28 Cr, 28 D, 28 E,	8 J, 8 Jr, 48 I
1 F, 1 G	**Lining** .... 5⅛ yds.
Fabric #14 .... ⅛ yd.*	**Batting** .... 62" x 89"
28 C	*See page 4.

1. Match fabric numbers to numbered colors shown on back cover of book. Referring to diagrams, make 25 Y blocks and six Z blocks as shown at right and on page 29. (By making each Z block different, you enhance the random effect and keep the colors balanced perfectly.)

2. Join Y blocks, I's, J's, and Jr's as shown below to make four Row 1's and three Row 2's, turning blocks every which way.

3. Join Row 1's and Row 2's alternately as shown in the photograph.

4. Mark quilting motifs given in A, I, J, and Jr patches. Referring to Fig. 1 on page 28, mark border quilting as follows: Mark motif from A patch in border with two leaves ¼" from inner seam line of border. Tip of one leaf should touch miter at corner. Mark 17 motifs, each 4¾" apart, in each long border. Mark 12 motifs, each 4½"

apart, in each short border. Mark scallops to connect motifs. Quilt as marked. Quilt "in the ditch" around patches. Bind to finish.

Block Y

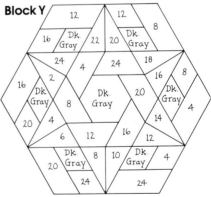

Block Y Piecing

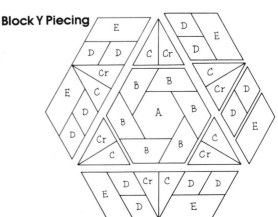

Row 1

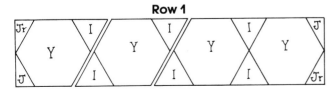

Row 2

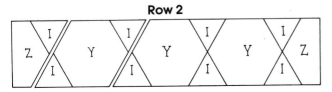

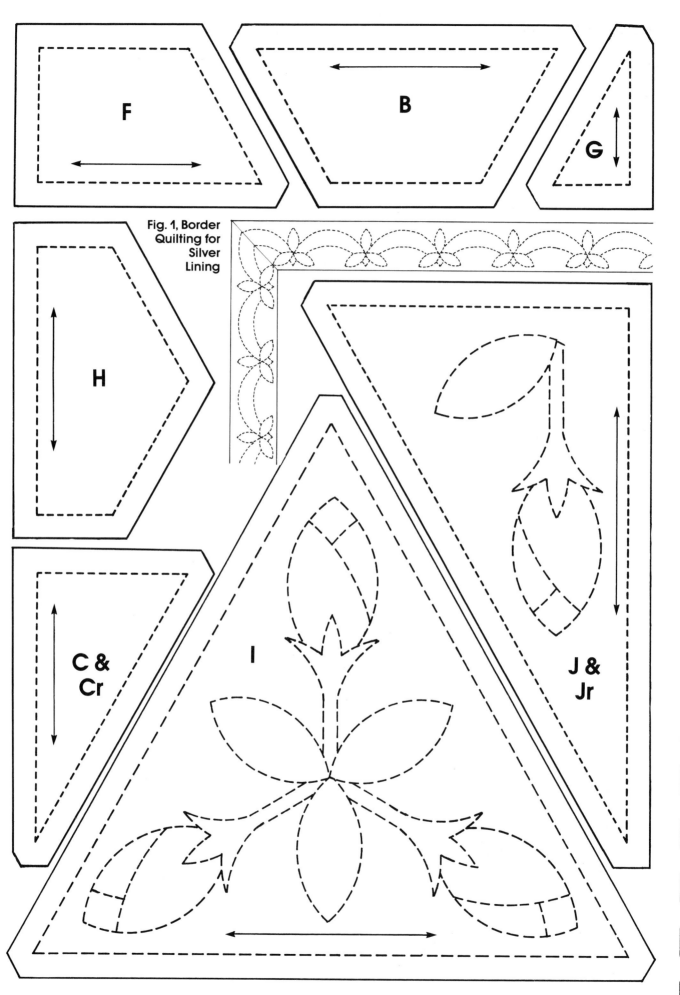

Fig. 1, Border
Quilting for
Silver
Lining

F

B

G

H

C &
Cr

I

J &
Jr

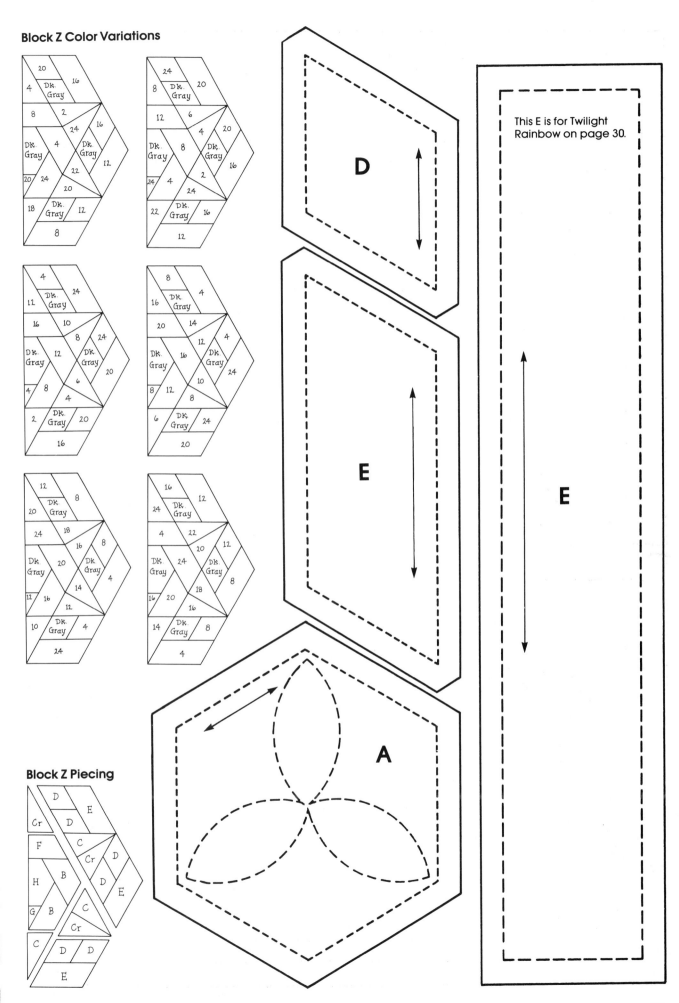

Block Z Color Variations

Block Z Piecing

D

E

This E is for Twilight Rainbow on page 30.

E

E

A

Twilight Rainbow

Stars twinkle in a rainbow of colors that march straight through the spectrum. The glorious border makes a fitting frame to a most handsome quilt. See the color photo on page 24.

Block Size: 9"	**Fabric #16**......... ⅛ yd.*
Quilt Size: 72" x 82½"	12 B, 12 Br
Fabric #1 .... ½ yd.	**Fabric #17** .... ⅜ yd.
66 A, 12 D	58 A, 14 D
Fabric #2 .... ⅛ yd.*	**Fabric #18** .... ⅛ yd.*
16 B, 16 Br	8 B, 8 Br
Fabric #3 .... ⅜ yd.	**Fabric #19** .... ⅜ yd.
54 A, 12 D	58 A, 12 D
Fabric #4 .... ⅛ yd.*	**Fabric #20** .... ⅛ yd.*
12 B, 12 Br	12 B, 12 Br
Fabric #5 .... ⅜ yd.	**Fabric #21**.......... ⅜ yd.
54 A, 14 D	56 A, 12 D
Fabric #6 .... ⅛ yd.*	**Fabric #22** .... ⅛ yd.*
8 B, 8 Br	8 B, 8 Br
Fabric #7 .... ⅜ yd.	**Fabric #23** .... ½ yd.
56 A, 14 D	66 A, 12 D
Fabric #8 .... ⅛ yd.*	**Fabric #24** .... ⅛ yd.*
12 B, 12 Br	12 B, 12 Br
Fabric #9 .... ⅜ yd.	**White**.............. 1¾ yds.
58 A, 14 D	272 A, 136 C
Fabric #10........ ⅛ yd.*	**Gray** .... 2¼ yds.
8 B, 8 Br	2 borders 2" x 67",
Fabric #11 .... ½ yd.	2 borders 2" x 56½",
70 A, 14 D	binding 1½" x 9¼ yds.,
Fabric #12......... ⅛ yd.*	5 sashes 2" x 51½",
12 B, 12 Br	24 E (pattern on pg. 29)
Fabric #13.......... ½ yd.	**Lining** .... 5 yds.
70 A, 14 D	**Batting** .... 76" x 87"
Fabric #14......... ⅛ yd.*	
16 B, 16 Br	
Fabric #15.......... ⅜ yd.	
58 A, 14 D	*See page 4.

1. Match fabric numbers to numbered colors shown on back cover of book. Referring to diagrams for O-Z, make blocks as shown. Unnumbered patches are white.

2. Set aside the four Z blocks. Arrange the remaining blocks, E's, and long sashes in rows as shown in the quilt diagram on page 31. Be careful to keep each block turned to match its block diagram. Pick up blocks and E's in order and stitch into rows. Join rows with long sashes between them.

3. Make borders as follows: Join remaining A's and D's to make 12 whole border units and two partial border units as shown below. Join three border units end to end for a border strip. Repeat to make four border strips. Sew a border strip to top of quilt. Repeat for bottom. Sew a partial border unit to the right end of each remaining border strip. Add a Z block to each end of these side border strips. Sew to sides of quilt.

4. Quilt "in the ditch" between patches. Bind to finish.

Border Unit

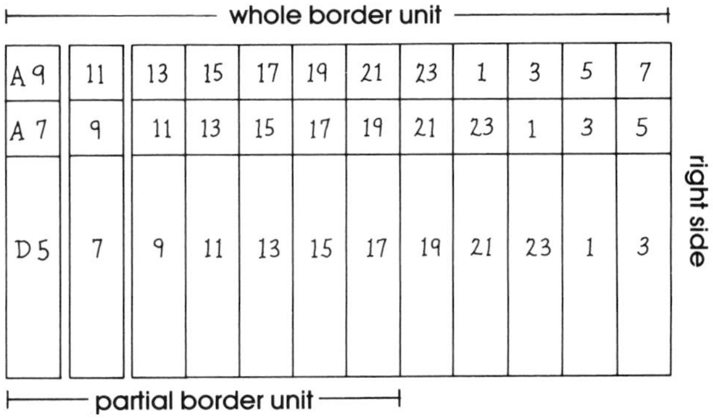

whole border unit											
A 9	11	13	15	17	19	21	23	1	3	5	7
A 7	9	11	13	15	17	19	21	23	1	3	5
D 5	7	9	11	13	15	17	19	21	23	1	3

partial border unit / right side

Block O: make 3

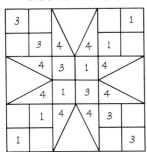

Block P: make 2

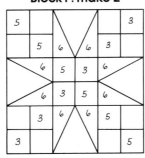

Block Q: make 3

Block R: make 2

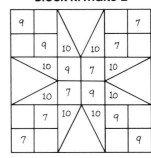

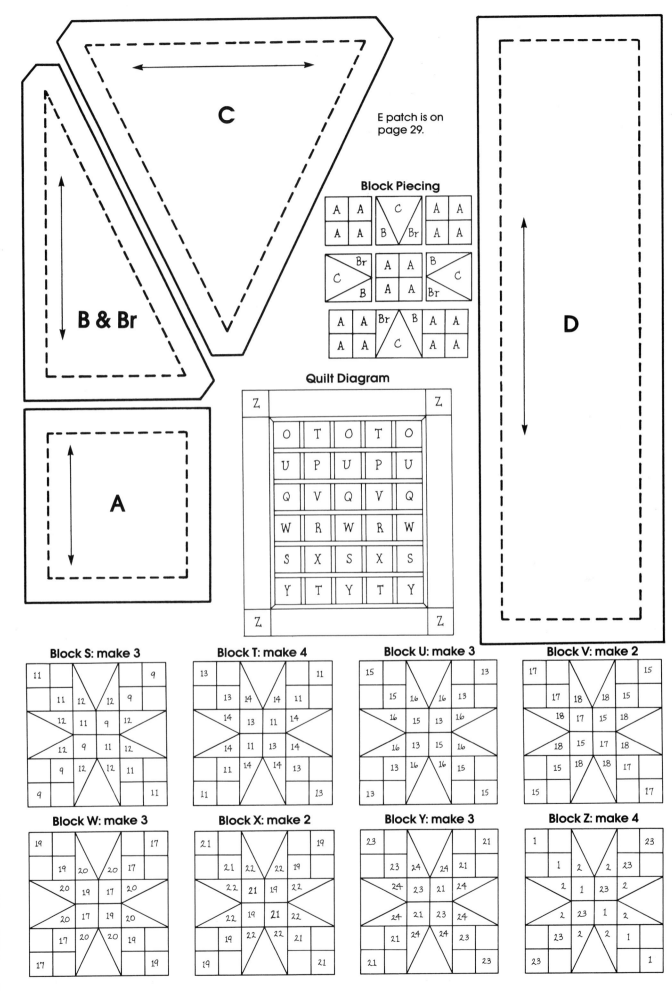

C

E patch is on page 29.

B & Br

A

D

Block Piecing

| A | A |
| A | A |

C / B | Br

| A | A |
| A | A |

Br / C / B

| A | A |
| A | A |

B / C / Br

| A | A |
| A | A |

| A | A | Br / C \ B | A | A |
| A | A | | A | A |

Quilt Diagram

Z					Z
	O	T	O	T	O	
	U	P	U	P	U	
	Q	V	Q	V	Q	
	W	R	W	R	W	
	S	X	S	X	S	
	Y	T	Y	T	Y	
Z					Z

Block S: make 3

11					9
	11	12	12	9	
	12	11	9	12	
	12	9	11	12	
	9	12	12	11	
9					11

Block T: make 4

13					11
	13	14	14	11	
	14	13	11	14	
	14	11	13	14	
	11	14	14	13	
11					13

Block U: make 3

15					13
	15	16	16	13	
	16	15	13	16	
	16	13	15	16	
	13	16	16	15	
13					15

Block V: make 2

17					15
	17	18	18	15	
	18	17	15	18	
	18	15	17	18	
	15	18	18	17	
15					17

Block W: make 3

19					17
	19	20	20	17	
	20	19	17	20	
	20	17	19	20	
	17	20	20	19	
17					19

Block X: make 2

21					19
	21	22	22	19	
	22	21	19	22	
	22	19	21	22	
	19	22	22	21	
19					21

Block Y: make 3

23					21
	23	24	24	21	
	24	23	21	24	
	24	21	23	24	
	21	24	24	23	
21					23

Block Z: make 4

1					23
	1	2	2	23	
	2	1	23	2	
	2	23	1	2	
	23	2	2	1	
23					1

Rainbow Ribbon Twist

Ribbons and rainbows weave a pretty spell in this strip-pieced bit of optical illusion. The large patches are quickly sewn and provide the perfect place to show off your quilting. A color picture is on page 25.

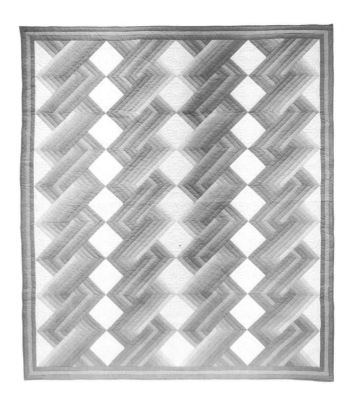

Quilt Size: 92⅜" x 103"	**Fabric #14**......... 2 yds.
Fabric #2 .... 1¼ yds.	binding 1½" x 11½ yds.,
14 strips 1¾" x 45"	14 strips 1¾" x 45"
Fabric #4 .... 1¼ yds.	**Fabric #16**....... 1¼ yds.
14 strips 1¾" x 45"	14 strips 1¾" x 45"
Fabric #6 .... 1¼ yds.	**Fabric #18**....... 1¼ yds.
14 strips 1¾" x 45"	14 strips 1¾" x 45"
Fabric #8 .... 2⅞ yds.	**Fabric #20** ...... 1¼ yds.
2 borders 1¾" x 100½",	14 strips 1¾" x 45"
2 borders 1¾" x 89⅞",	**Fabric #22** ...... 1¼ yds.
14 strips 1¾" x 45"	14 strips 1¾" x 45"
Fabric #10......... 3 yds.	**Fabric #24** ...... 1¼ yds.
2 borders 1¾" x 103",	14 strips 1¾" x 45"
2 borders 1¾" x 92⅜",	**Cream**............ 1⅞ yds.
14 strips 1¾" x 45"	27 B, 18 C
Fabric #12......... 3 yds.	**Lining** .... 8¼ yds.
2 borders 1¾" x 105½",	**Batting** .... 96½" x 107"
2 borders 1¾" x 94⅛",	
14 strips 1¾" x 45"	

1. Match fabric numbers to numbered colors shown on back cover of book. First make strip-pieced Unit 1's. Referring to Fig. 1, join strips to make nine panels as shown. Cut two A's from each panel. This gives you 18 Unit 1's.

2. Next, make Unit 2's. Referring to Fig. 2, join strips to make nine panels as shown. Cut two A's from each panel to make 18 Unit 2's.

3. For Units 3 and 4, refer to Fig. 3. Make five panels as shown. Use the C template to cut 18 each of Unit 3 and Unit 4.

4. For Units 5 and 6, refer to Fig. 4. Make five panels as shown. Use the C template to cut 18 each of Unit 5 and Unit 6.

5. Also cut 27 B and 18 C from cream solid.

6. Join B's, C's, and units as shown to make a row. Make nine rows. Join rows, being careful to turn every second row with the opposite edge up.

7. Add borders, mitering corners and trimming excess from seam allowances.

8. Mark and quilt the motifs given in cream B and C patches. Quilt as marked and quilt "in the ditch" between patches. Bind to finish.

Fig. 1

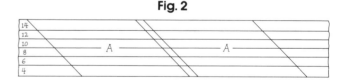

Fig. 2

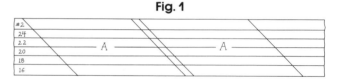

Fig. 3

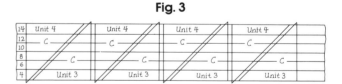

Fig. 4

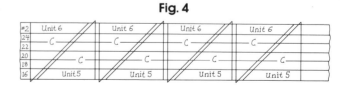

Row

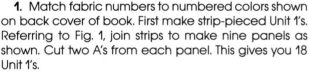

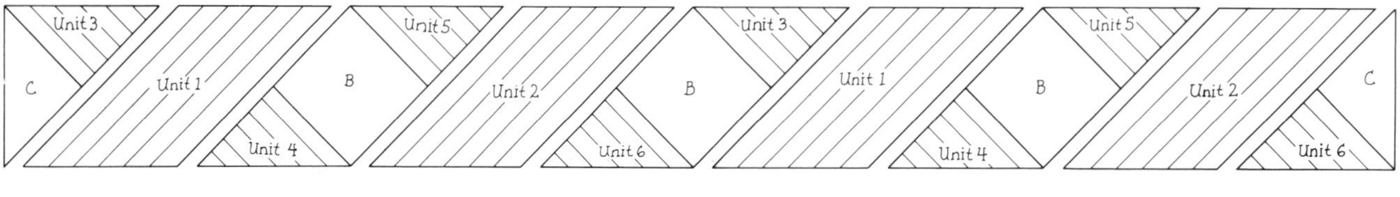

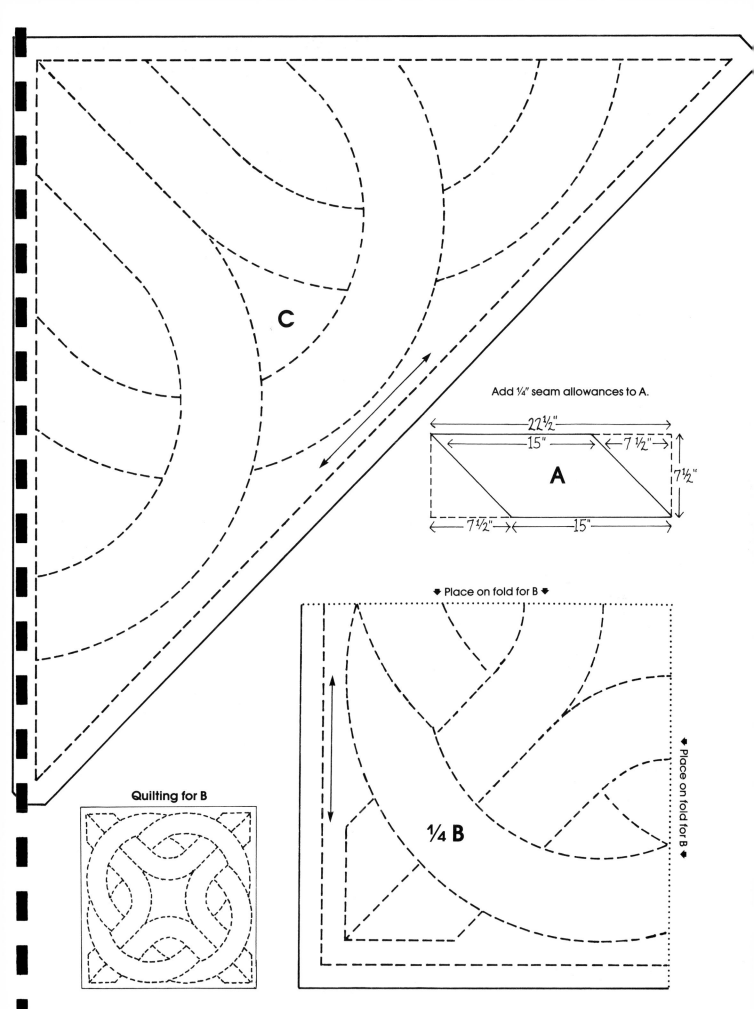

C

Add ¼" seam allowances to A.

22½"

15"   7 ½"

A

7½"

7½"   15"

◆ Place on fold for B ◆

◆ Place on fold for B ◆

¼ B

Quilting for B

Rainbow Weave

Subtle color shifts and an overlay of curved quilting lines give this extra-easy quilt a delightfully complex look. Color photo is on page 26.

Block Size: 7"	Fabric #14........... 1 yd.
Quilt Size: 71¾" x 99¾"	binding 1½" x 10 yds.,
Fabric #1 .... ¼ yd.*	20 A
18 A	Fabric #15........ 3 yds.
Fabric #2 .... ½ yd.	2 borders 3⅛" x 102¼",
19 A	2 borders 3⅛" x 74¼",
Fabric #3 .... ¼ yd.*	23 A
18 A	Fabric #16.......... ½ yd.
Fabric #4 .... ½ yd.	20 A
19 A	Fabric #17 .... 2¾ yds.
Fabric #5 .... ¼ yd.*	2 borders 2¼" x 97", 2
18 A	borders 2¼" x 69", 18 A
Fabric #6 .... ½ yd.	Fabric #18.......... ½ yd.
19 A	19 A
Fabric #7 .... ¼ yd.*	Fabric #19.......... ¼ yd.
18 A	18 A
Fabric #8 .... ½ yd.	Fabric #20 .... ½ yd.
19 A	19 A
Fabric #9 .... ½ yd.	Fabric #21......... ¼ yd.*
23 A	18 A
Fabric #10.......... ½ yd.	Fabric #22 .... ½ yd.
20 A	19 A
Fabric #11 .... ½ yd.	Fabric #23 .... ¼ yd.*
23 A	18 A
Fabric #12.......... ½ yd.	Fabric #24 .... ½ yd.
20 A	19 A
Fabric #13.......... ½ yd.	Lining .... 6 yds.
23 A	Batting .... 76" x 104"

3. Add borders, mitering corners and trimming excess from seam allowances.

4. In light-colored blocks and borders, mark and quilt random curving lines as shown in the photograph. Quilt "in the ditch" around blocks. Quilt ¼" from seam lines along long edges of rectangles in the dark blocks. Bind to finish.

1. Referring to diagrams below, make 23 U blocks, 18 V blocks, 18 W blocks, 20 X blocks, 19 Y blocks, and 19 Z blocks. Blocks can be made by strip-piecing sets of four 2¼"-wide strips and cutting panels into 7½" blocks (to finish 7") if you prefer.

2. With blocks turned to match the diagrams, join into six rows of nine as shown in the six-row diagram. Repeat. Join the two sections. Make another row like the top row and sew it to the bottom of the quilt.

Block U

9
11
13
15

Six-Row Diagram

U	X	U	Z	U	Y	U	X	U
Z	V	Y	V	X	V	Z	V	Y
W	X	W	Z	W	Y	W	X	W
Z	U	Y	U	X	U	Z	U	Y
V	X	V	Z	V	Y	V	X	V
Z	W	Y	W	X	W	Z	W	Y

*See page 4.

A

Block V

17
19
21
23

Block W

1
3
5
7

Block X

10	12	14	16

Block Y

18	20	22	24

Block Z

2	4	6	8

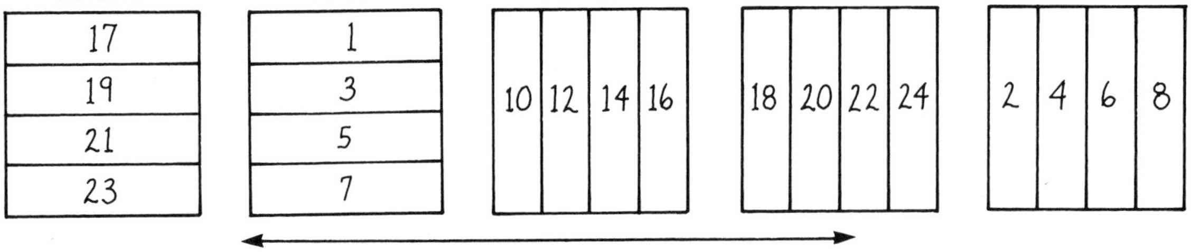

Match fabric numbers to numbered colors shown on back cover of book.

More Patterns

Here and on the next five pages are full-size patterns for the 20 quilt blocks shown in color on pages 2 and 43. The letters in the patterns correspond to the letters in the piecing diagrams on pages 41-42. Pattern pieces are presented in alphabetical order, organized according to shape, so you can find any one easily. In order to conserve space, some of the squares and triangles have been presented superimposed over larger patches of the same shape. When you trace the larger patches, be sure to include the part that is "over-lapped" by the smaller patches. Seam allowances are included, with points trimmed to help you align the patches for machine piecing. Arrows on patches should be aligned with the straight grain of fabric, preferably lengthwise although crosswise is acceptable. Basic quiltmaking instructions are on pages 4-5. Suggestions for making quilts from these patterns are given under each piecing diagram. Feel free to use any of the patterns to make pillows or to make quilts in sizes or arrangements that are different from those listed.

> **✳** Ten quilts, each of which can be made from a rainbow packet of 24 "fat quarters" (18" x 22"), are indicated by asterisks under their piecing diagrams. Fabric in contrasting colors for alternate blocks, sashes, and background patches may be required in addition to the rainbow colors. As well, many small projects, such as pillows, can be made from a quarter yard or less of each rainbow color.

Squares

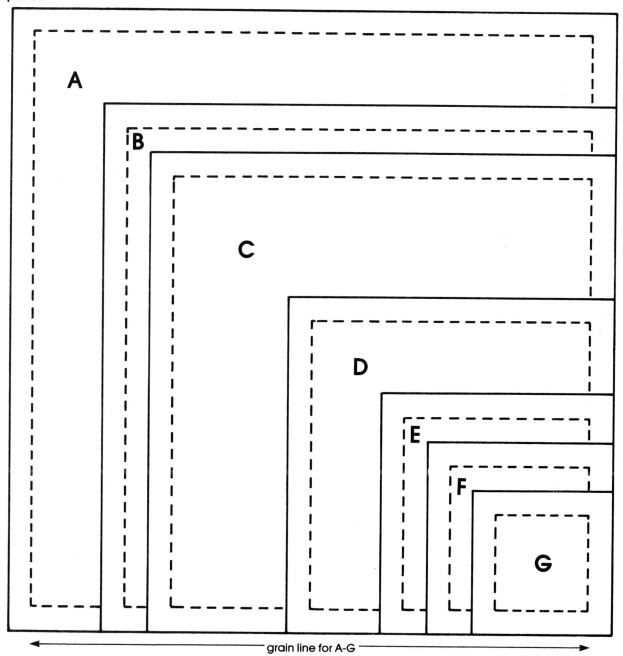

grain line for A-G

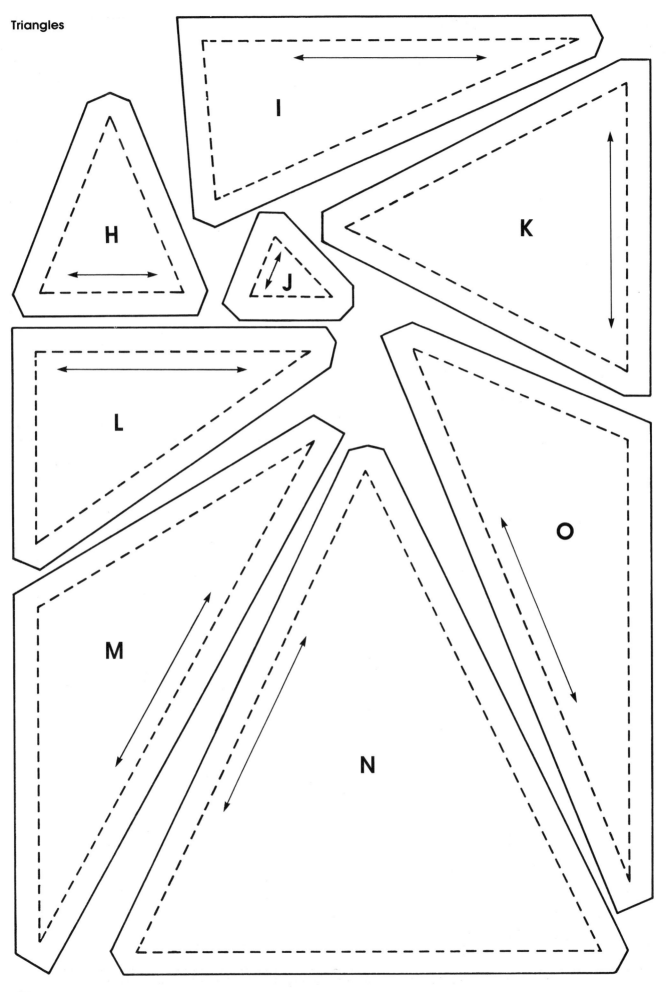

Triangles

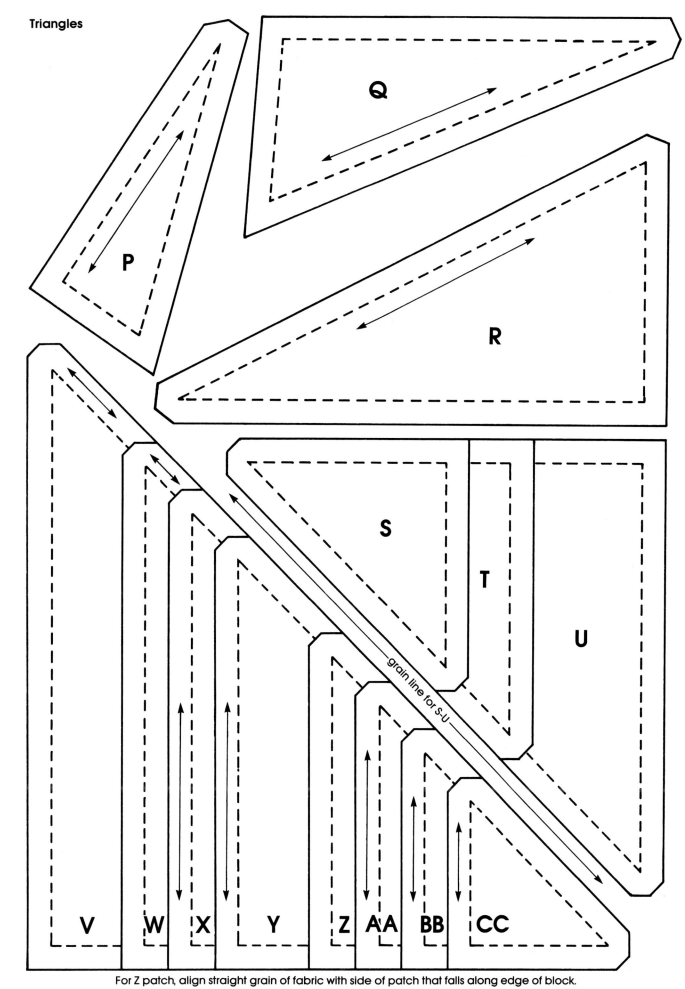

Q

P

R

S

T

U

grain line for S-U

V   W   X   Y   Z   AA   BB   CC

For Z patch, align straight grain of fabric with side of patch that falls along edge of block.

37

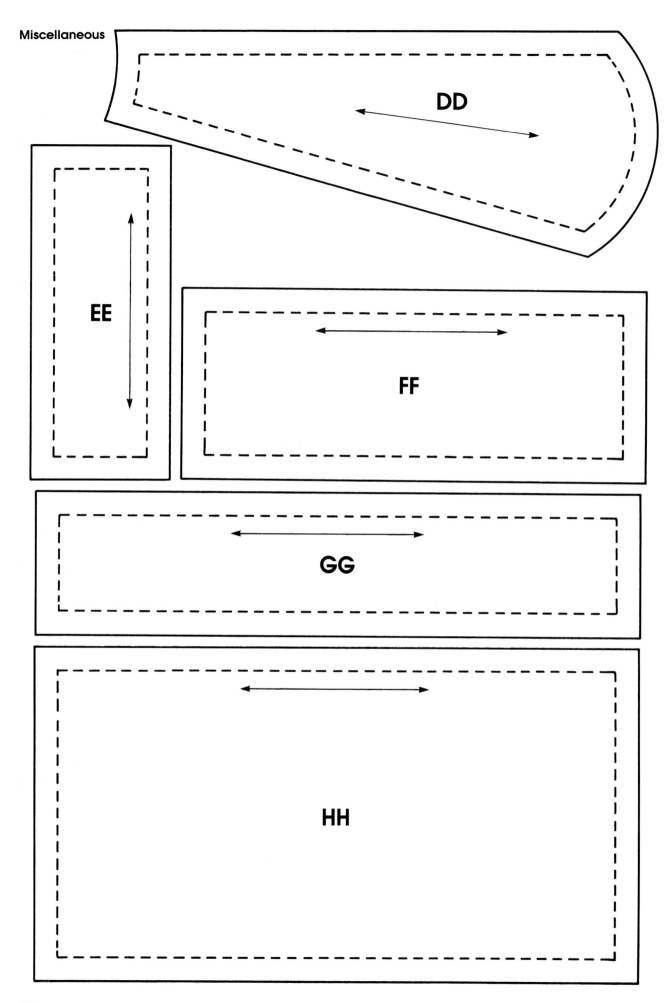

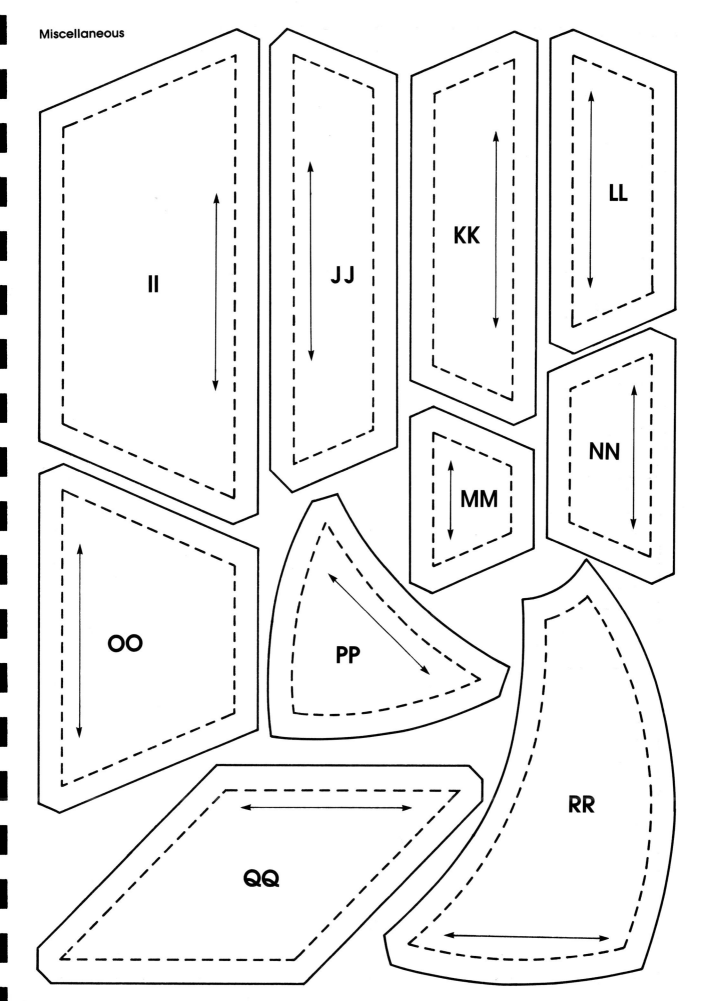

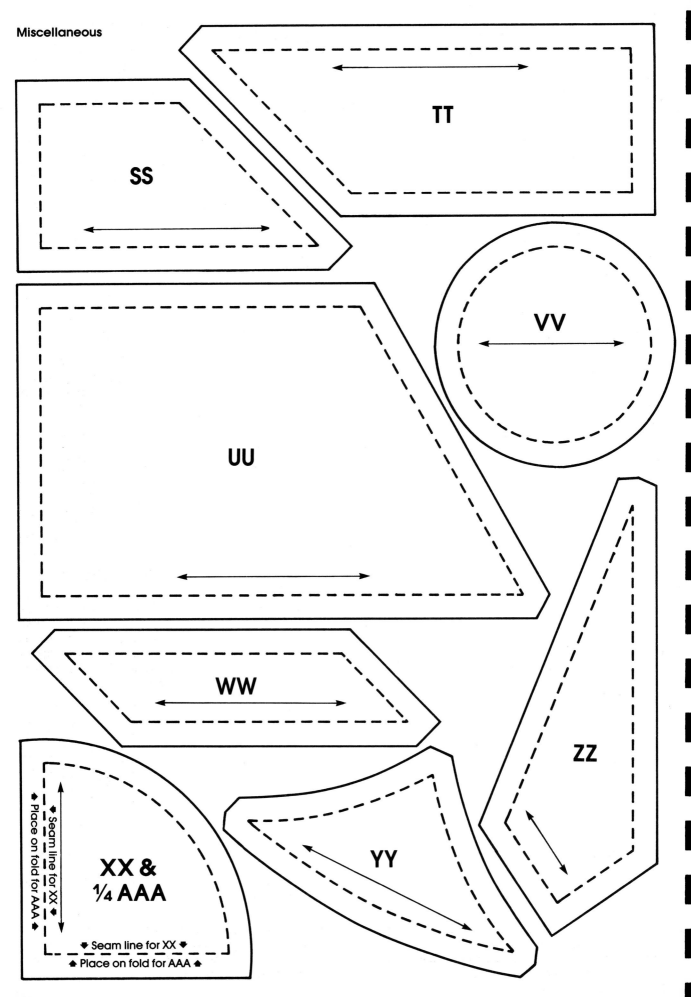

SS

TT

UU

VV

WW

ZZ

YY

XX &
¼ AAA

Place on fold for AAA

Seam line for XX

Seam line for XX

Place on fold for AAA

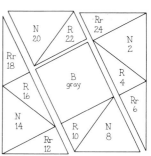

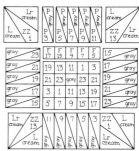

Golden Gate, 16½". 20 blocks set 4 x 5 with 3" sashes make a quilt 81" x 100½".

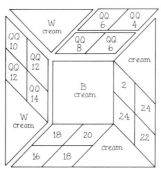

Around the Chimney, 11¼". 56 blocks set 7 x 8 make a quilt 78¾" x 90".

Delaware Crosspatch, 11¼". 48 blocks set 6 x 8 make a quilt 67½" x 90".

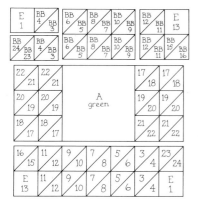

Indian Plumes, 14". 30 blocks set 5 x 6 with 2" sashes make a quilt 82" x 98".

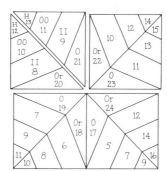

Riviera, 12". 48 blocks set 6 x 8 make a quilt 72" x 96".

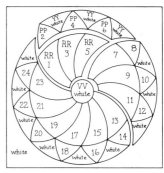

The Thorny Thicket, 11". 48 blocks set 6 x 8 with 2" sashes make a quilt 80" x 106".

Exploding Stars*, 9". 13 blocks set alternately with 12 plain squares in 5 rows of 5 make a wall quilt 45" x 45".

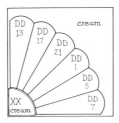

Grandma's Fan*, 8". 24 blocks set 4 x 6 make a quilt 32" x 48". Join DD's, add XX, then appliqué to 8" (finished) background square.

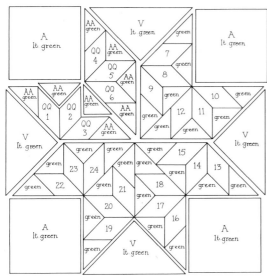

Flying Swallows*, 20½". 20 blocks set 4 x 5 make a quilt 82" x 102½".

*See page 35.

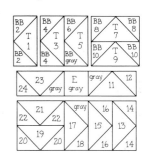

Feathered Star*, 13". 18 blocks set alternately with 17 plain squares in 7 rows of 5 make a quilt 65" x 91". Appliqué onto 13" (finished) background square.

Flying Geese*, 10". 35 blocks set 5 x 7 with 2" sashes make a quilt 62" x 86".

The piecing diagrams on this page correspond to the quilt blocks shown in color on page 2. Letters signify pattern pieces; numbers indicate colors. See color wheel on the back of the book to match actual fabrics to the numbers listed. Full-size patterns for making these quilts are on pages 35-40. Suggested quilt sizes and arrangements are listed; however, feel free to change the sizes or arrangements as you like.

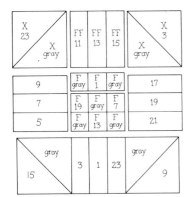

Path and Stiles, 13½". 30 blocks set 5 x 6 with 3" sashes make a quilt 85½" x 102".

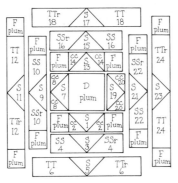

Priscilla's Dream, 12". 32 blocks set alternately with 31 plain squares in 9 rows of 7 make a quilt 84" x 108".

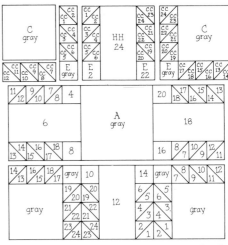

Texas Treasure*, 18". 9 blocks set 3 x 3 make a quilt 54" x 54".

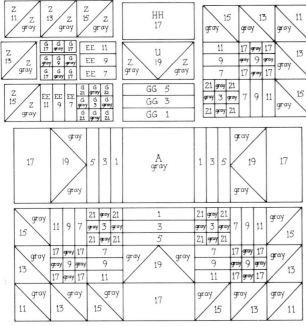

Nebraska, 24". 9 blocks set 3 x 3 with 3" sashes make a quilt 84" x 84".

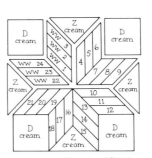

Liberty Star*, 10¼". 35 blocks set 5 x 7 with 3" sashes make a quilt 69¼" x 95¾".

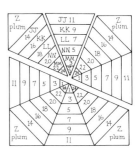

Spider's Web*, 10¼". 12 blocks set 3 x 4 make a quilt 30¾" x 41".

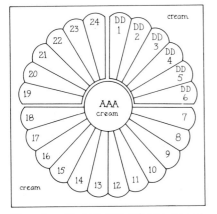

Dresden Plate*, 16". 20 blocks set 4 x 5 with 2" sashes make a quilt 74" x 92". Appliqué plate on 16" (finished) square.

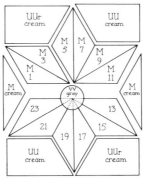

Old Colony Star*, 10⅜" x 12". 36 blocks set 6 x 6 with 2" sashes make a quilt 76¼" x 86". The circle is appliquéd over the completed star.

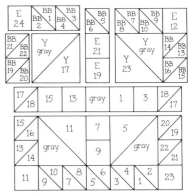

Prickly Pear, 14". 18 blocks set alternately with 17 plain squares in 7 rows of 5 make a quilt 70" x 98".

*See page 35.

The piecing diagrams on this page correspond to the quilt blocks shown in color on page 43. Letters signify pattern pieces; numbers indicate colors. See color wheel on the back of the book to match actual fabrics to the numbers listed. Full-size patterns for making these quilts are on pages 35-40. Suggested quilt sizes and arrangements are listed; however, feel free to change the sizes or arrangements as you like.